DRIED & TRUE

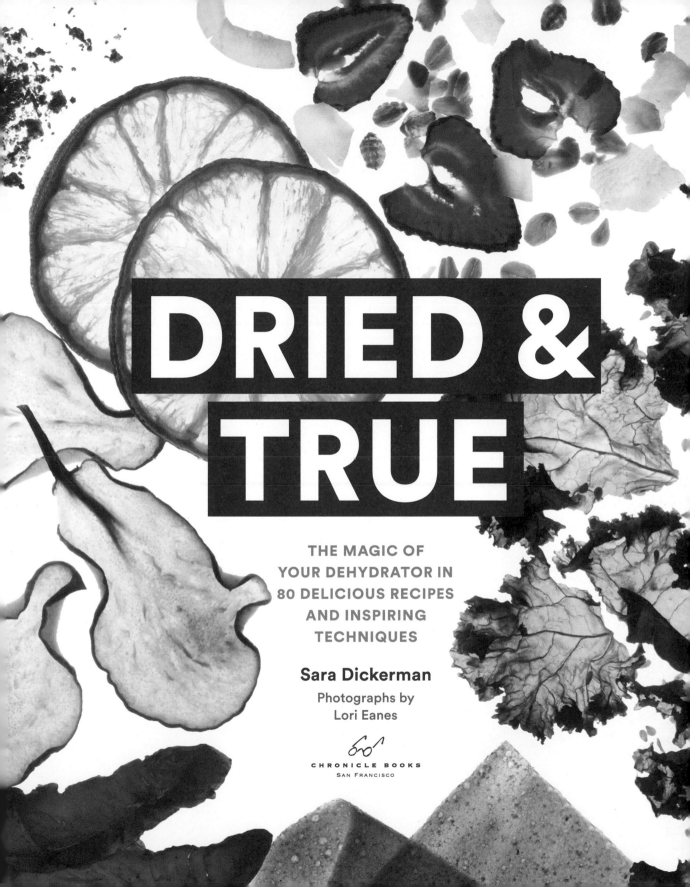

DRIED & TRUE

THE MAGIC OF YOUR DEHYDRATOR IN 80 DELICIOUS RECIPES AND INSPIRING TECHNIQUES

Sara Dickerman

Photographs by
Lori Eanes

CHRONICLE BOOKS
SAN FRANCISCO

Text copyright © 2016 by Sara Dickerman.
Photographs copyright © 2016 by Chronicle Books LLC.

Library of Congress Cataloging-in-Publication Data:
Names: Dickerman, Sara 1971- author.
Title: Dried & true : 80 big-flavored dehydrator projects for fruits,
vegetables, powders, jerky, and more / Sara Dickerman.
Other titles: Dried and true
Description: San Francisco : Chronicle Books, [2016] | Includes index.
Identifiers: LCCN 2015039650 | ISBN 9781452138497 (pbk. : alk. paper)
Subjects: LCSH: Cooking (Dried foods) | LCGFT: Cookbooks.
Classification: LCC TX826.5 .D53 2016 | DDC 641.6/14--dc23 LC record
available at http://lccn.loc.gov/2015039650

Manufactured in China

MIX
Paper from
responsible sources
FSC
www.fsc.org
FSC™ C008047

Designed by Alice Chau
Photographs by Lori Eanes
Food styling by Randy Mon

Chronicle books and gifts are available at special quantity discounts to
corporations, professional associations, literacy programs, and other
organizations. For details and discount information, please contact our
premiums department at corporatesales@chroniclebooks.com or at
1-800-759-0190.

10 9 8 7 6 5 4 3 2 1

Chronicle Books LLC
680 Second Street
San Francisco, California 94107
www.chroniclebooks.com

CONTENTS

INTRODUCTION

This book is a guide to using a home dehydrator creatively. I had long been a fan of dried fruit and beef jerky, but I purchased them from grocery and specialty stores. Eventually I began to see ambitious chefs incorporating dried elements into their work, from flavorful powders to little nuggets of chewy fruits and vegetables. I got curious and proposed an article on the subject to my editor at Slate, and acquired my first food dehydrator. I played around with drying strawberries, cherries, and even watermelon. I continued to experiment with drying herbs, meats, fish, vegetables, fruits, and even flowers, and I shared ideas with friends for how to best use their dehydrators.

I found that most sources of information on dehydration were less playful than I like to be in the kitchen. I wanted a book full of bold flavors, timely ingredients, and fun ideas for presentation. And so I wrote this book. In these pages, I cover the basics: Preparation, drying, and storage of almost any food you might think of drying. The recipes also invite you to do more, to harness the dehydrator not just as a practical tool but as a means to delightful results. With its help, you can make such items as pesto powder and citrus sugar, elegant vanilla pear slices and kid-pleasing fruit leathers, rustic chipotle jerky and hearty dried mushroom soup for backpacking. I'm confident you'll discover—as I have—that the food dehydrator can be a winning and versatile kitchen addition.

DRYING FOOD

Is it sunny as you read this? Is there a gentle breeze stirring? If so, you have what it takes to dry food, because Earth's atmosphere is the oldest, largest dehydrator there is. Drying food as a means of preservation is older than history, no doubt older than agriculture itself. Somewhere along the way, a Stone Age hunter happened to chew on a leathery strip of old meat, and beef jerky was born. And the first raisins were probably a cluster of shriveled wild grapes that some gatherer picked and stored for future use.

Simple as it was, the calculated drying of food items was a huge development; it was a bet on the future and a premeditated act of planning. Drying made it possible to extend a healthful diet beyond the immediate stages of a fresh kill or a windfall of fresh edible plants. When food is purged of most of its moisture, it no longer provides a good habitat for the rascally strains of bacteria, yeasts, and molds that can ruin it. (Some microbes, however, do help preserve food through the process of fermentation.) Dried food is also lighter and thus more portable than moist food, helping to ensure nutrition even as people traveled and explored new territories.

Drying is still a major means of preserving food. Rice, seafood, pasta, grains, legumes, meats, fruits, spices, and vegetables are all still commonly dried for storage in countries around the world. The majority of the world's population still survives without a home refrigerator, so without dried food, there would be a constant struggle against spoilage.

Throughout history, drying processes became more complex and efficient. People discovered that fruits and vegetables dried more quickly if elevated off the ground by even a rustic mesh of branches. They learned that dairy could be dried too. In the thirteenth century, Marco Polo observed Tartar armies drying milk in the sun, so they could carry the resulting powder with them on their journeys. People also found that fish and meat dried better and more safely with the addition of salt. And smoke was often used as a part of the drying and preservation process of fish and game.

Today there are several mechanical means of drying food. Industrial techniques like freeze-drying work to very efficiently preserve food. Freeze-drying systems first freeze food, and then warm it gently, under very low air pressure. In this environment, the ice in these foods turns into a gas, skipping the liquid stage. The process leaves behind a crunchy, structurally sound version of the dried food—like uncannily crisp peas and raspberries—which can be simply rehydrated by soaking in water. Unfortunately, such freeze-drying systems aren't designed or priced with the home cook in mind; they cost thousands of dollars.

Old processes such as heat (like the sun) and air circulation (like the wind) are still used as well. Commercial facilities have large dryers that pass warm air over apricots and apples or strips of meat en route to jerky. The most straightforward versions of these dryers simply vent damp air away from the drying chamber like a clothes dryer does; others cool and recirculate the air with a heat pump.

Our home food dehydrators are simply more compact versions of the hot-air and venting method. They come in a few shapes and sizes, but all rely on the circulation of warm air to draw moisture away from ingredients to dry them. Because the technology is relatively simple and inexpensive, we are lucky; we can use dehydrators for an expansive variety of at-home food projects. This book will focus on just that, from basics like dried apricots to more involved projects like lamb jerky.

It is ironic, perhaps, that I would be writing a book about dehydration. Rainy Seattle, where I live, isn't a place where you typically think of things drying out. If you take a look at the U.S. government's Mean Annual Relative Humidity map, my home in Seattle sits in the middle of a green splotch, indicating annual humidity average of about 73 percent, about twice that of Phoenix. But I consider my hometown's lack of aridity a good test—it means that if I can make amazingly tasty snacks, meals, and edible gifts with my home dehydrator, then you can too.

If you happen to live in Phoenix, you'll just be able do it more swiftly.

I came to dehydration as a skeptic. Why would I want to dry my own foods when grocery stores all around me sell beef jerky, fruit leathers, and dried fruit galore? There is no driving *need* for me to dry my own food. I'm not a raw foodist, so I'm not concerned about the temperature at which my food is prepared. I don't have, say, an apple orchard that would require my saving vast quantities of produce. I don't backpack often enough to require dried meals in great quantities.

In my case, the line between need and pleasure is consistently blurred. And when used with a spirit of curiosity and fun, the food dehydrator delivers big on delight. Working at home, with the best foods I can grow or purchase, I am able to get an incredibly wide range of fresh, intense flavors with my dehydrator. Fresh herbs are transformed into vivid seasoning powders, grass-raised beef and lean buffalo make for the most flavorful jerky I've ever tasted, and crunchy little seeds can be made into satisfying crackers and granolas (many of which are gluten-free, too!).

I'm not alone in using dehydrators to make familiar ingredients into something new. Modern chefs are making candied tuiles out of fruits and vegetables for dramatic, crispy garnishes. They are powdering hand-foraged herbs and dusting plates with dramatic speckles of green, and drying seafood to make homemade versions of classic Chinese sauces. Though it's not the flashiest tool in today's highly technical kitchens, the dehydrator helps the cook explore flavor and textural variation.

I do have some practical reasons for using a dehydrator as well—it's a great tool for preserving the season. As I write this paragraph, apricots are just coming into full flush in our markets, and I know I can save them for the future by putting them in the dehydrator today. Later on, I may decide to make pan de higo, the Spanish-inspired fruit and nut pâté, which is heaven with a wedge of Manchego cheese. Or I may make orange blossom–scented apricots to top my morning yogurt.

Dehydrators also help reduce waste in my kitchen. I get perfectly crisp bread crumbs from any stale bread I process. I'm always ready to make the kids some crunchy cheese-crusted chicken. I can also dry any leftover risotto so we have it on hand the next time we go camping. And I can dry leftover meat scraps for dog treats.

When I'm not eating bread crumbs and am trying to cut back on refined carbohydrates in my diet, the dehydrator lets me make a pile of low- or no-grain treats, sweetened, if at all, with agave syrup or honey. For snacks, I can make crispy kale chips and flaxseed crackers, airy zucchini chips and butternut squash slivers, and nutty strawberry-coconut muesli. This book is written for folks on general well-balanced diets, but it's filled with recipes that will delight gluten-free, Paleo, vegan, or vegetarian eaters.

And, of course, dehydrators are a great boon for creating backpacking foods. Water is a key source of weight in food, and eliminating moisture means seriously reducing pack weight. Though the main focus of this book is not backpacking recipes, I have included a few to get you started—scalloped fingerling potatoes that rehydrate into a most delicious breakfast dish, nutty quinoa spiked with chunks of red bell peppers, and tasty lemon hummus for the road.

My dehydrator is a wonderful source of adventure in my kitchen. I use drying alongside pickling, jam making, and freezing to keep the freshness of each season close at hand. Though the electricity that runs my dehydrator is a modern development, I love to reflect on the age-old history of the method.

I hope you'll join me in exploring the many tastes and textures that are simple to create with this ancient approach to preserving food.

CHOOSING A DEHYDRATOR

You can try your first dehydrating experiments in a home oven, setting it to the lowest possible temperature (preferably with the convection fan on, if your oven has that feature). Improvise a drying rack by setting a cooling rack atop a baking sheet. With this approach, your food will dry quicker than in a dehydrator and may be quite crispy in some spots, but it is a fun way to get started. Soon, though, you'll likely want to invest in a home dehydrator, which will provide more control and even results.

Home dehydrators combine a circulating fan with heating elements to heat food from approximately 95° to 165°F [35° to 74°C]. Inside, they have several layered trays made of plastic or metal that allow warm air to circulate around food and hasten evaporation, so the food dries evenly without overbrowning.

You'll want a dehydrator with adjustable temperature control, and I really appreciate having a timer setting on the machine. Since dehydration takes a long time, it's handy to have the machine turn itself off at 2 A.M., rather than needing you to do it.

STACKING DEHYDRATORS

The most commonly used food dehydrators are round, stacking countertop machines. In this variation, the heating and fan unit sits on top of a stack of donut-shaped trays that you fill with ready-to-dry food. Warm air flows around the perimeter of the trays and across the food on the trays. A drip tray at the bottom catches all the juices. Nesco is the most popular maker of this type of dehydrator.

The smaller units, which are about the size of a big cake-box, are relatively inexpensive. These models have several distinct advantages: They are small and light. You can increase the capacity of your machine by simply purchasing additional stacking trays (the manufacturer's instructions advise you on the number of trays you can use with regard to the wattage of your dehydrator's drying unit). The trays have pronounced edges, so roly-poly foods like cherry tomatoes don't roll off as you're carrying them. Accessories like fruit-leather drying sheets and mesh drying sheets are cheap and easy to come by; they also have a lip on them, to contain liquid foods like soup or tomato sauce. And the stacking trays are small and relatively easy to clean. Though it's not officially sanctioned, I will run especially sticky trays through the dishwasher on an express setting to get a really thorough wash, but you should avoid the hot drying cycle.

The disadvantage of these round stacking machines is the donut shape of the trays, which doesn't offer a lot of drying area. And if you're making fruit leather, it's hard to spread the fruit out evenly in these trays and to cut it into regular pieces.

RECTANGULAR BOX DEHYDRATORS

If you are willing to step up in price, you will find rectangular box dehydrators with fully removable trays (the most common brand is Excalibur). They take up more room in your kitchen (they are about the size of a small microwave oven but lighter), and their capacity is set; the most common model has nine trays, though larger and smaller units are available. The individual rectangular trays can accommodate more food than donut-shaped trays can, which is great if you're working with ingredients like orange rounds or fennel slices. If you're making a fruit leather, the rectangular batch can be easily cut into even strips.

These box-like machines have the heater/fan unit on the back, so you don't need to lift the unit as you're rotating trays or pulling out a finished batch (like with the round stacking dehydrator). This design also offers a more even distribution of heat throughout the machine, so you don't need to rotate trays as much. (But because heat rises, you still need to rotate trays at least once during the drying process to get even results.)

Excalibur dryers also have a fluctuating heat cycle during operation rather than the continuous cycle found in other dryers. When the temperature cools a bit during drying, the manufacturer says that the interior moisture moves toward the exterior. And when the heat picks up again, external moisture is evaporated at a quicker pace. In theory, this minimizes toughening while drying.

In the basic Excalibur system, trays are plastic with fine poly-mesh inlays that keep little berries from falling through. (In the circular-tray systems, the holes are bigger, though you can purchase finer-mesh liner sheets for smaller items). The mesh inlays are handy because you can roll them as you tip your food into a container, funneling all the loose bits without a mess.

The poly-mesh screens aren't made for high-temperature sanitizing, which you might want to do if you're working on a lot of jerky. Stainless-steel dehydrators with metal trays are available, which can be boiled or steamed to aid in the cleaning process, but they are more expensive. These durable steel machines are heavier than plastic models.

If you're setting up a business, you can consider all sorts of dehydrator upgrades: higher-volume machines, ones with two temperature zones, and, of course, freeze-drying units that render food almost instantly crisp and dry. But the automobile-level pricing on some of these machines is just too much to consider for most home users.

ACCESSORIES AND TOOLS

Like all good hobbies, food dehydration can draw you into wanting to use some serious accessories and tools, some more crucial than others. You don't need everything on this list to get started, but these items have served me well in my dehydrating kitchen.

AIRTIGHT CONTAINERS

Once you get into dehydrating, you'll start collecting containers for storing your dehydrated foods. You can never have enough.

Mason, Bell, and Weck jars are an attractive way to store your dried goods. And glass is advised for storing acidic foods. You'll be tempted to display your dried items in the kitchen window, but they'll last longest if you keep them in a dark cupboard.

Spice jars are perfect for powdered food items. The best ones have a rubber or silicone airtight seal in the lid.

Vacuum bag systems are very effective for packaging because they are heat sealed and they automatically remove extra air before sealing.

Ziptop plastic freezer bags (and small ones for backpacking) are effective and easy to use, and they store compactly. Press extra air out of each bag for stacking.

BLENDER

A large blender, particularly a high-speed, large-capacity blender (like a Vitamix) can quickly make purées and pulverize dried ingredients into powder.

CANDY THERMOMETER

I use a hot sugar-syrup method for my dehydrator meringues, which is much easier to do with a thermometer adapted for high-heat environments. You should be able to find a candy thermometer in your grocery housewares aisle, cooking supplies stores, or online.

CHERRY PITTER

You really need a cherry pitter only if you're going to dry cherries (or maybe olives)—if that's your plan, you will be glad to have one. I use a small handheld model that looks a bit like a stapler; but if you really do a lot of cherries, you can seek out a countertop lever-action cherry pitter (or cherry stoner).

FOOD MILL

A hand-cranked food mill is a useful low-tech tool for making smooth purées for fruit and vegetable leathers, especially if you want a finer texture. The screen at the bottom separates tough skins and large seeds from the pulp, making a very smooth purée.

FOOD PROCESSOR

A large food processor can be very handy in the home dehydrating kitchen. With a large motor and sharp blades, it can mince meat, slice or shred vegetables almost instantly, powder dried ingredients, and purée fruit for leathers. However, it is less convenient for grinding, chopping, or puréeing small batches.

JERKY GUN

This specialized tool is for making jerky from minced meat, and it's especially useful for producing a large amount of it. I find it both handy and fun. A jerky gun works like a caulking gun; it extrudes the seasoned meat out onto the nonstick sheets in neat ribbons or cylinders. For this purpose, you could also use a dedicated pastry bag with a flat tip.

LABELER

My husband jokes that I am obsessed with my labeler, but if you get into serious drying, it's a very good idea to have a labeling system. You can use an electronic labeler like I do, or just use tape and a Sharpie to mark each of your projects with the contents and the date.

MANDOLINE

Basically a flat tool with a sharp slicing edge running across the center, a mandoline is a fantastic, easy-to-clean tool for evenly slicing fruits or vegetables. Inexpensive plastic models are good for items like cucumbers, apples, pears, onions, and fennel. I like the even-cutting V-shaped blade of the Swissmar Borner mandoline. Sturdy metal mandolines, like the Bron slicer, are ideal for stickier, starchier vegetables such as potatoes, sweet potatoes, and celery root. When using a mandoline, remember to use the fingertip guard that comes with the tool so you don't cut your fingertips.

MICROPLANE AND OTHER GRATERS

Rasp-like graters, such as a Microplane, produce fine shavings of fresh citrus zest or cheese that will dry quickly in the dehydrator. The fine holes on a box grater also work well, but make sure your grater is still sharp (if not, it may be time for a replacement).

NONSTICK FRUIT-LEATHER SHEETS

If you are going to work with sticky foods like fruit leathers, you'll need to stock up on liner sheets for your dehydrator trays. Don't use wax paper, which will fall apart in the drying process. If you're working with a Nesco-style round dehydrator, you can buy extra fruit-leather sheets to line the trays. These are supersmooth, donut-shaped plastic disks that can hold liquid or semiliquid foods like fruit purées or soups as you dry them. If you are working with a square dryer, Excalibur makes great ParaFlexx-coated sheets that fit over the poly-mesh screens in their trays. You can also use the more durable silicone baking mats—like the Silpat brand—for the same purpose; just make sure the mats are sized to fit your dryer trays. It is also handy to keep one of these nonstick sheets at the bottom of your dehydrator to make cleaning the machine easier.

NONSTICK MESH SHEETS

Most round stacking dryers come with extra mesh sheets, but eventually you'll probably want to get a few more of these easy-to-clean screens, which line the trays and keep small bits of food from falling through the holes. If you purchase a square Excalibur-style dehydrator, which comes with trays already lined with poly-mesh screens, you may still want to purchase a few extra screens.

NOTEBOOK AND PEN

You will want to record the time and temperature of your drying projects so that you can best adapt your dehydrator to your own climate and techniques. I like to keep my notebook on top of the dehydrator, so if I add some extra drying time to a project, I don't forget to record it.

OFFSET SPATULA

This pastry tool is really helpful if you're making a lot of fruit leathers and need to spread the purées out neatly and evenly.

PEELERS

Peelers are great both for removing skins and for making thin, easy-to-dehydrate strips of lemon peel, asparagus, carrot, and parsnip. I favor Y-shaped peelers, and replace them every year or two so that they are always sharp enough to do my bidding.

RULER

If you want your jerky or your apple slices to dry as evenly as possible, keep a small ruler in your tools to make sure you are cutting or shaping items evenly before processing.

SHORT-BRISTLED BRUSH

This tool is essential for cleaning dehydrator screens and trays. I also use a pot-scrubbing brush, and a toothbrush-style brush with short, flexible bristles to get between cracks and into crevices.

SILICA GEL PACKETS

These mysterious little packets are often in the box when you buy a new pair of shoes. They're filled with moisture-absorbing silica crystals. They're especially helpful in keeping powders from clumping up and warding off mold. I started off just hoarding them from packages I happened to find them in, and now I order them online. There are also oxygen-absorbing packets on the market that further extend storage life of dried foods, but their use is more complicated. If you become deeply involved in long-term storage of your dried food, you may want to learn about those.

SPICE GRINDER

The one tool you'll find indispensable for preparing foods for dehydrating is a spice grinder. My spice grinder is actually an inexpensive coffee grinder dedicated to spice use. Its small size and sharp, rapidly turning blades are ideal for small batches of lightweight ingredients. But if you don't have a spice grinder and you run across a recipe that calls for one, you can use other tools like a mortar and pestle, a blender, or a food processor.

SPIDER

A spider is a long-handled tool with a wide wire-net scoop at the end. It is my preferred tool for fishing blanching items out of a pot of hot water. They are inexpensive and can be found in Asian markets, kitchen supply stores, or online. You can also use a large slotted spoon or a strainer to do the job.

STEAMER

Although you can use a large pot of boiling water to blanch vegetables and fruit before dehydrating, steaming is also an effective method as well, which some people prefer (see Blanching, page 21).

TIMER

It can be very handy to have more than one timer on hand while you are drying. You can track your drying time on one close to the dehydrator, and carry another one with you if you roam away from the machine and need a reminder to turn it off at a certain time.

KEYS TO SUCCESSFUL DEHYDRATING

Dehydrating takes patience. Dehydration is a slow process, but it's easy, fun, and well worth it. Following are some general tips for success.

HUMIDITY AND MOISTURE

Humidity varies greatly across the country, from my damp hometown of Seattle to the arid mountains of New Mexico to the moist Atlantic seacoast. Fruits and vegetables also vary greatly in moisture content; you might have a juicy apple or a starchy one, and a winter plum tomato from Mexico will be considerably less moist than your summer garden heirlooms. If you're drying a huge batch of plums, your dehydrator will get full of moisture, so a machine full of plums will take longer to dry than a single tray of them.

GIVE YOURSELF TIME

Dehydrators vary widely from model to model in working characteristics. The standard round stacking dehydrators are very convenient in terms of size, price, and availability, but they work more slowly than the larger, enclosed metal units with bigger fans. When you get in the drying habit, you will adapt to these variables. Just make sure to be prepared for your projects and give yourself time to complete them.

DON'T GET STUCK

In addition to using fine-mesh sheets on drying trays, as extra insurance, I also usually coat the sheets with a thin layer of cooking oil. I initially used nonstick cooking spray to coat the trays.

Be careful to do this in the sink or over a tray you don't mind getting oily. Just spraying a tray or sheet in the air can make for a slippery mess on the floor—something I learned from experience. Eventually, I decided that I preferred greasing the trays with a paper towel soaked in olive oil, a neutral oil like canola or grapeseed, or a sweet flavorsome oil like almond oil. It seemed less messy and avoided introducing any propellants into our atmosphere.

There are also several accessories to use alone or in addition to oil to help prevent sticking. For example, if you are making jerky with ground meats, or if you want to make small individual portions of fruit leather, you can purchase strips of coated paper about 3 in [7.5 cm] wide, which can be used in either round or rectangular dehydrators.

Commercial-style dryers may have stainless-steel trays, which food items tend to stick to more than they do to nonstick plastic versions. For this kind of dryer, you'll want to take extra care greasing the trays and will likely want to invest in mesh sheets and/or nonstick fruit-leather sheets to lay atop the steel for smaller or more liquid items.

CHOOSING THE RIGHT SPOT FOR THE DEHYDRATOR

My dehydrators live in the basement. This is somewhat inconvenient, since I often have to run downstairs carrying awkward trays of, say, grapes that threaten to roll off at any moment. But dehydrators are a little noisy; they make about the same amount of noise as a kitchen hood fan. Depending on what you are drying, they can also emit odors. If you're drying a batch of pineapple, the whole room can smell fragrant like a tropical tiki bar, but if you're making homemade garlic powder, you may not *want* the dehydrator nearby. So if you can put your dehydrator somewhere other than your main living/sleeping area, you may want to do so. If you choose to put it in a cellar or garage, make sure that area is clean and dry.

CHOOSING THE RIGHT FOODS

Only select food that is in great shape for drying. Dehydrating will not improve food that is past its prime. I make a point of drying with the seasons, shopping for big batches of good-looking, fresh, firm, ripe ingredients as they show up in the markets and making sure they aren't bruised or concealing any bugs or rot.

Frozen fruits and vegetables can also be dried, either as part of a purée for fruit leather, or individually if the items are small, like berries or corn kernels. If you don't have the time or inclination to dry your market-fresh fruit in midsummer, you can freeze it on baking sheets before transferring it to freezer bags for longer storage (and then dehydrate it later, if you wish).

PREPARING FOODS FOR DRYING

Wash and dry any fruits or vegetables before dehydrating. In the case of garden-fresh food, also take care to pick out any damaged produce and undesired leaves, stems, or bugs before drying.

Wash foods in a cool water bath. Strain them and dry, in a salad spinner if appropriate, or lay them out on a clean kitchen towel to absorb any surface moisture.

SPACING OUT FOOD ITEMS ON TRAYS

When you lay out foods on drying trays, give them plenty of headspace so they will dry evenly. Slicing ingredients evenly also helps to unify your drying time for a certain type of food. In the recipes, I do not give a specific number of trays to use for each product, since different dehydrators have different dimensions, but keep in mind that you will get the quickest and most even drying if you lay out your ingredients in a single layer, leaving a good perimeter of space—*at least* ½ in [1 cm]—between morsels of food. In general, I recommend preparing two trays, laying out the ingredients, and then proceeding with more trays if needed. Also take time to rotate trays during drying to ensure the most even drying conditions; some dehydrator manuals say this is unnecessary, but it's best to do it. Follow your individual dehydrator's recommendation for the minimum number of trays to place in the dryer, even if not all of them are holding ingredients.

JUDGING DONENESS

Dried foods can have many different textures, and as you use your dehydrator more, you will learn how to gauge the right texture. The Dehydration Chart for Common Foods on page 160 and the recipes give approximate drying times for various foods, and they also give textural descriptions so you can decide for yourself when foods are done. A piece of jerky should be dry, matte, but still a bit flexible when it is done; a sprig of basil should be completely dry and crisp. Because sugar is hydrophilic (it tends to bond with water), foods with sugar in them tend to take longer to dry and may not become completely crisp, hence the telltale chewiness of raisins or dried apricots. So, if you add sugar or other sweeteners to the food item you are drying, such as in the Bananas Foster Trail Mix (page 135) or the Dried Orange Cranberries (page 53), keep in mind that it will add to the drying time.

The good news is that although dehydration takes a while—from about 3 hours for bread crumbs and some herbs to 3 days for whole dried chile peppers or figs—the dehydration process doesn't require much active involvement. Say you're waiting for some fruit to dry and it takes longer than expected. You've watched some late-night TV, but you really want to go to sleep. Do not be dismayed! If your project is not completely dry, you can turn off the dehydrator for the night and then start it again in the morning. You may find that your ingredients have dried just right with residual evaporation overnight. If not, turn on the dryer again.

Alternatively, you can turn the heat way down for overnight dehydration. This kind of slow drying is especially effective when you want to minimize the surface hardness on your food items; you don't want a fig, for example, that is leathery outside but still completely moist and squishy inside.

IF YOU GO TOO FAR

It is possible to dry plums or tomatoes until they are too hard to chew easily. If so, don't panic. You can place overdried foods on the stove top in a pot fitted with a steamer rack or basket over about 2 in [5 cm] of boiling water. Steam for 5 to 10 minutes until they soften to the preferred texture. Or you can place the item in a microwave-proof bowl with 2 to 3 Tbsp water, cover securely, and microwave in 30-second bursts until the food has softened.

CLEANING UP

Cleaning the trays can sometimes be challenging, and one advantage of the metal dehydrators is that their stainless-steel trays fit well in the dishwasher. Though it is not recommended by the manufacturer, I confess that I frequently place my plastic drying trays in the dishwasher, on the express setting, which doesn't superheat the plastic on the drying cycle. But with hot soapy water and a stiff brush, it doesn't take long to clean the trays by hand, which is the best solution for long-lasting dehydrator trays.

STORING THE RESULTS

Because the recipes in this book do not use artificial preservatives, the shelf life of the dried foods may not be as long as commercially dried products. In general, I recommend eating what you dry within two weeks of putting it up, but this is not a hard-and-fast rule. If you are drying moist fruit or veggies to use later, then conditioning your ingredients before permanent packaging is a good idea (see Methods to Improve Your Dehydrating, facing page).

Dried food keeps well in airtight containers in a dark environment (like a cupboard) at cool or room temperature. Including a silica gel packet along with the dried food will extend freshness. If you want to really extend the life of your dried foods, you can always put them into the freezer. This works well for moister foods, since crispier dried foods can lose their texture in the fridge or freezer.

Throughout the book, I will give you conservative estimates for storage times for particular dehydrated foods. Don't automatically toss your food on the far end of my estimate. I am giving you suggestions for the ideal timeline for eating your dried food, not necessarily for how long it will be edible. I encourage you to use your own observations for judging whether your dried food is in good shape. Here, are some pointers for judging the condition of your stored dried food.

Strange smells and flavors: If your dried food smells bad or tastes off, especially in the case of dried meat, it has become rancid or gotten moldy. Toss.

Sweatiness: If there's a lot of moisture collecting in your food container after the first two or three days of storage (when moisture levels may just be evening out), then you may be headed for spoilage. Put this dried food in the fridge or freezer.

Mold: Mold is a definite sign of spoilage. I tend to toss the whole batch only if I see that it's moldy all over. If I spot just one bad piece of fruit, I throw that away and monitor the rest of the batch carefully.

Loss of flavor: Flavor can leach out of your dried food after time, especially if the food is not stored in the dark. This is most likely to happen with herbs, garlic, and other powders. Once it does, toss and make a new batch.

METHODS TO IMPROVE YOUR DEHYDRATING

Dipping

You don't need to pretreat foods before drying them. Some items, however, like apples or peaches, get brown from exposure to oxygen on their cut surfaces, and they will become less brown during drying if you dip them in a solution of citric acid, which is the powdered form of the acid found in lemon juice. (I choose not to use sodium bisulfate, the color-preserving additive in many commercially dried fruits, since some people are allergic to it.) You can source citric acid at many health food and drug stores, or online. When preparing a batch of such foods for drying, make a solution of 1 tsp citric acid for each 1 qt [960 ml] water in a large bowl, and then drop in the foods and let soak for a couple of minutes. Drain as well as possible and place on your prepared trays. Or you can use a one-to-one ratio of lemon juice to water, but that requires a lot of lemons!

Blanching

Blanching is the process of briefly immersing your food items in boiling water to halt enzyme actions that can cause loss of flavor, color, and texture. After blanching, the ingredients should be removed to an ice-water bath to quickly stop the cooking. This method is useful for several food items. For example, when blanched, spinach and tender herbs retain their bright green color and will dry faster. The process cracks the waxy skins of tough-skinned fruits like grapes, cranberries, tomatoes, figs, and blueberries and exposes the flesh of the fruit to the circulating air in the dehydrator. You can also use a steamer basket to blanch foods.

Conditioning

When you dry food that you want to be semimoist (like chewy dried fruit), some pieces will retain more moisture than others. Before sealing them up for long-term storage, you can take a step called *conditioning* to even out the moisture. Place some of the cooled, dried items into an airtight jar, and agitate it daily for five or six days. Look for significant moisture gathering in the container; if you see it, you may need to return the food to the dehydrator. After a conditioning period, the food should be evenly moist. Then, you can seal it really well, preferably with a silica gel packet to extend freshness.

REHYDRATING

You can rehydrate most dried foods by putting them in a bowl, covering with boiling water, and letting them soak for about 15 minutes. Depending on the food, you may want to incorporate the soaking liquid into your finished dish (mushroom soaking liquid, for example, can be used as the broth in the dish). You can also use a steamer to rehydrate foods.

PREPARING RAW OR LIVING FOODS

Many of the recipes in this book can work for raw-food diet protocols. But they will take longer at the very low temperatures used in drying. You'll also probably want to work with smaller, thinner pieces of food to streamline drying at those low temperatures.

CHAPTER 1:
FLAVOR
BOOSTERS

A great way to make your cooking at home more compelling is by layering flavors. I always use plenty of herbs, chiles, citrus peel, onions, and garlic in my cooking. And I have discovered that the food dehydrator can reveal and enhance flavor complexities in herbs and other flavoring elements.

Perhaps my most delightful discovery in working with home dehydration has been the deliciousness of homemade flavor powders, salts, and sugars. Here's the idea: Take fresh cremini mushrooms, slice them, and dry them in your dehydrator. When completely dry, pulverize them in a spice grinder and mix with a little salt or sugar (or nothing else). Sprinkle the mushroom powder into other foods, such as hamburger meat or a pot of simmering soup, for a deliciously intense flavor boost. You can make flavor powders with anything from apples to chiles, veggies to herbs. Some food powders, such as powdered beets and spinach, can also be used as natural food colorings.

The flavor boosters in this book do not taste the same as the dried herbs or seasonings you get at the grocery store. When you work with the freshest ingredients and dry them yourself, you'll find that you will be packing much more intense flavor into a little jar.

Take a simple example—garlic powder. I'm strictly a whole-foods cook, and I had long ignored garlic powder at the grocery store. But one day, I remembered my mother's delicious roast beef that always relied on a sprinkling of garlic powder. And the more I read about barbecue, I noticed that many of America's finest BBQ pitmasters rely on the stuff. Turns out, garlic powder doesn't burn as readily as fresh garlic, so it's perfect for food items that are going to be cooked for a long time. So I sliced up a couple of heads of peeled garlic cloves and set to drying them. It took about 18 hours, but when they were crisp and dry, I ground them up in my spice grinder. The next time I cooked a roast, it was as tasty as my mother's. I found I had a secret weapon for my future roasts and barbecues. It was well worth the effort.

In this chapter, we'll get even trickier, making everything from pesto dust to rose sugar to top your next batch of cupcakes. Not only are these flavorful powders a great addition to your own kitchen, but if you package them in a pretty jar or a whimsical test tube, they make terrific gifts as well.

Here is the basic method for making your own garlic powder. Following it is a variation, my take on my mother's roast beef seasoning. I give the mixture a huskier tone with the addition of one of my kitchen staples: smoked paprika. Besides using it on roast beef, you can also try it on roast chicken or add it to sautéed onion when you season chickpeas for a side dish. You could even use it on oven-roasted tofu for your next quick vegetarian meal.

BASIC GARLIC POWDER

MAKES ABOUT ⅔ CUP [75 G]

4 heads garlic cloves, peeled and thinly sliced

1 tsp fine sea salt

1. Line dehydrator trays with non-stick mesh sheets that have been lightly coated with cooking oil.

2. Lay out the garlic slices on the prepared trays. **Dry at 125°F [52°C] for 15 to 20 hours**, until the garlic slices are completely dry and crack when bent. Let cool completely.

3. In a spice grinder, working in batches, pulverize the garlic to a very fine powder, adding about ½ tsp salt to each batch to help prevent sticking. (To prevent the grinder from jamming, start grinding with the grinder upside down and then turn it right-side up.)

4. Store in an airtight container, preferably with a silica gel packet to extend freshness, in a dark place at room temperature for up to 6 months.

MOM'S ROAST BEEF SEASONING, SMOKIFIED

Mix together 2 Tbsp Basic Garlic Powder, 2 tsp smoked paprika, 4 Tbsp kosher salt, and 2 tsp freshly ground black pepper. Store in an airtight container, preferably with a silica gel packet to extend freshness, in a dark place at room temperature for up to 6 months.

MAKES ABOUT ½ CUP [60 G]

A turmeric tonic is one of those folk remedies that can make me feel alive when I've got a head full of congestion or a sore throat. I use this powder in the beverage recipe that follows, in which turmeric tastes quite delicious in an intensely golden way, especially if you use a generous hand with the honey. You could also add this ocher-yellow powder to your next curry for a burst of turmeric flavor that's much more delicious than what you can get from a store-bought spice jar.

TURMERIC-GINGER-LIME POWDER

MAKES ABOUT ⅓ CUP [20 G]

1 lime

3 oz [85 g] fresh turmeric root, peeled and thinly sliced

2 oz [60 g] fresh ginger root, peeled and thinly sliced

1. Line dehydrator trays with non-stick mesh sheets that have been lightly coated with cooking oil.

2. Using a peeler, remove just the bright green zest of the lime peel. (Reserve the rest of the lime for another use, including, if desired, a spritz in the finished brew.)

3. Lay out the lime zest strips and the slices of turmeric and ginger in a single layer on the prepared trays. **Dry at 135°F [57°C] for 6 to 8 hours**, until the turmeric and ginger slices are crackly dry. Let cool completely.

4. In a spice grinder, pulverize the lime zest, turmeric, and ginger to a fine powder.

5. Store in an airtight container, preferably with a silica gel packet to extend freshness, in a dark place at room temperature for up to 6 months.

TURMERIC-GINGER-LIME ZINGER

When I traveled to Bali, I was regularly offered a refreshment of turmeric, ginger, lime, and honey, and here I've re-created the beverage in an easy-to-brew concoction. Place ¾ tsp Turmeric-Ginger-Lime Powder into a mug. Add 1 cup [120 ml] boiling water and stir to dissolve. Stir in 1 tsp honey, or more to taste. Brighten with a squeeze of fresh lime juice, if desired, before serving. If you want an extra dose of sinus-clearing power, stir the tiniest wisp of cayenne pepper into your drink.

MAKES 1 DRINK

Kimchi, a spicy Korean fermented cabbage often used as a condiment, is surprisingly versatile when dried. These days, you can purchase fresh, prepared kimchi at most supermarkets with deli counters, like Whole Foods. After drying the kimchi, you may leave it in its leafy state, ready to add tang, heat, and a little chewy texture to your packaged backpacking meals. For at-home use, I dry the kimchi and then make it into a powder, which I use as an umami-packed flavor booster for noodle soups, rice porridge, mashed potatoes, even quesadillas. I especially love to supercharge Dijon mustard with kimchi powder. It's like combining the forces of all the best hot dog toppings—sauerkraut, mustard, chile peppers, and relish. Kimchi styles vary greatly in texture and chile heat, so pick a kimchi that tastes good to you in its refrigerated state before drying.

KIMCHI POWDER

MAKES ABOUT ¼ CUP [40 G]

1 cup [210 g] prepared kimchi, drained

1. Line dehydrator trays with non-stick mesh sheets that have been lightly coated with cooking oil.

2. Lay out the kimchi in a thin layer on the prepared trays. **Dry at 135°F [57°C] for 12 to 18 hours,** until the kimchi is brittle and completely dry to the touch. Let cool completely.

3. In a spice grinder, working in batches, pulverize the dried kimchi into powder.

4. Store in an airtight container, preferably with a silica gel packet to extend freshness, in a dark place at room temperature for up to 2 months, or in the freezer for up to 1 year.

KIMCHI MUSTARD

Mix 2 Tbsp of Kimchi Powder into ½ cup [120 ml] high-quality Dijon mustard (I like Fallot). Transfer to an airtight jar and let sit in the refrigerator to allow the flavors to meld for at least 1 day. Stir to blend. Store in the refrigerator for up to 6 months.

MAKES ABOUT ½ CUP [85 G]

There's no such thing as too much basil. But in the final days of summer, even home gardeners can end up with more basil than we can cope with at once. Drying is a great solution. I'm always surprised by how vivid the flavor of the basil is when I dry it myself. Blanching the herbs beforehand helps keep the leaves vivid green, and—weirdly—shortens their drying time. When working with fresh herbs, keep the leaves on their stems, since this is the easiest way to handle them once dried. I grind the basil leaves into a pesto-inspired finishing powder that can wake up eggs, beans, simple grilled fish, and, of course, pasta. Add in some extra-virgin olive oil, Parmigiano-Reggiano cheese, and toasted pine nuts for a delicious summery dish in any season.

PESTO DUST

MAKES ABOUT ½ CUP [60 G]

8 oz [230 g] basil sprigs

2 garlic cloves, peeled and grated

2 tsp finely grated lemon zest

1 tsp fine sea salt

⅛ tsp freshly ground black pepper

1. Line dehydrator trays with non-stick mesh sheets that have been lightly coated with cooking oil.

2. Bring a large pot of salted water to a boil over medium-high heat. Meanwhile, fill a large bowl with ice water.

3. Drop half of the basil sprigs into the boiling water, and push down with a slotted spoon to submerge. Cook until the leaves wilt and turn a darker shade of green, about 20 seconds. With the slotted spoon, transfer the basil directly into the ice water. Repeat with the remaining basil.

4. Spread out the garlic thinly on one prepared tray.

5. When the basil is cool, squeeze gently to remove excess water and place on the prepared trays. Dry at 135°F [57°C] for 4 to 5 hours, until the basil is dry and crisp. Let cool completely.

6. Pluck off the basil leaves and put them in a medium bowl. Add the dried garlic, lemon zest, salt, and pepper and stir to combine. In a spice grinder, working in batches, process the mixture into a fine powder.

7. Store in an airtight container, preferably with a silica gel packet to extend freshness, in a dark place at room temperature for up to 3 months.

This all-purpose powder delivers a big wallop of umami, a taste that gives food a meaty or savory flavor. It's my secret agent for burgers and meatloaf, for memorable soups and wintry pots of beans. Every now and then, when I'm organized enough, I gather some sea lettuce from the beach and dry that along with the mushrooms. But usually, I use a little bit of packaged nori (seaweed), which couldn't be simpler.

UMAMI DUST

MAKES ABOUT 1½ CUPS [170 G]

8 oz [230 g] shiitake
mushrooms, stemmed

8 oz [230 g] cremini or button
mushrooms, stemmed

2 sheets toasted nori or
1 cup [85 g] wild fresh
edible seaweed, rinsed

1 tsp fine sea salt

1. Line dehydrator trays with non-stick mesh sheets that have been lightly coated with cooking oil.

2. Lay out the caps of the shiitake mushrooms on the prepared trays, either side facing up. Cut the cremini mushrooms into ½-in [12-mm] slices and lay out on the prepared trays. If working with fresh seaweed, also lay it on the prepared trays. **Dry at 125°F [52°C] for 12 to 14 hours**, until everything is completely dry and crispy. Let cool completely.

3. Tear the nori into small pieces and put in a medium bowl. Add the dried mushrooms and salt and stir to combine. In a spice grinder, working in batches, pulverize the mushroom mixture into a fine powder. (To prevent the grinder from jamming, start grinding with the grinder upside down and then turn it right-side up.)

4. Store in an airtight container, preferably with a silica gel packet to extend freshness, in a dark place at room temperature for up to 3 months.

UMAMI BUTTER

Recently, I had some Umami Dust sitting unused in the pantry and decided to combine it with one of the most savory preparations in this book, Dried Caramelized Onions (page 90). I mixed these two flavor powders together with some butter and a bit of raw garlic and, when I painted it on the skin of a just-roasted chicken, I couldn't believe the intensity of those flavors working together. It also goes well spread on veggies and even toast. Mix 2 Tbsp room-temperature butter with 1 grated garlic clove; 2 Tbsp Umami Dust; and 1 Tbsp Dried Caramelized Onions, ground into powder.

MAKES ¼ CUP [65 G]

Black olives dried in the dehydrator take on a novel texture and taste; crisp like shards of potato chips but rich with their own wine-dark flavor. Use as a finishing flourish atop crudités, grilled fish, or your next tuna casserole.

DRIED BLACK OLIVE CRUMBLE

MAKES ABOUT 1 CUP [100 G]

2 cups [400 g] pitted, coarsely chopped Kalamata olives

2 tsp finely grated lemon zest

1. Line dehydrator trays with non-stick mesh sheets that have been lightly coated with cooking oil.

2. In a medium bowl, toss the olives with the lemon zest to combine. Lay out the mixture on the prepared trays. **Dry at 135°F [57°C] for 10 to 14 hours**, until the olives are dry and crunchy. Let cool completely.

3. Roughly chop the olive mixture again.

4. Store in an airtight container, preferably with a silica gel packet to extend freshness, in a dark place at room temperature for up to 3 months.

I'm no teetotaler, but I'd rather have a Virgin Mary than a real Bloody Mary. I love the sweetness of onion and tomato together, accented with the brisk pinch of horseradish, pepper, and celery. Somehow I just don't need the additional sensation of vodka. (But, hey! Combine Bloody Mary mix with beer to make a Michelada, and that's another story.) This flavor booster recipe conjures all those flavors in dried form. It's a great seasoning for eggs or retro canapés (cream cheese and celery, anyone?), and, of course, it's ideal for rimming the glass of a delicious Bloody Mary, with or without the booze.

BLOODY MARY SALT

MAKES ABOUT ⅓ CUP [35 G]

1 medium shallot, peeled and cut into ¼-in [6-mm] slices

2 medium tomatoes, cut into ⅛-in [3-mm] slices

1½ tsp prepared horseradish

Finely grated zest of 1 lime

4 tsp fine sea salt

1 tsp Worcestershire sauce

1 tsp sugar

½ tsp ground black pepper

⅛ tsp celery seeds

¼ tsp cayenne pepper

1 Tbsp flaky sea salt

1. Line dehydrator trays with non-stick mesh sheets that have been lightly coated with cooking oil. Have one dehydrator tray outfitted with a nonstick fruit-leather sheet.

2. Lay out the shallot and tomato slices on the mesh-lined trays. On the tray with the nonstick fruit-leather sheet, spread out the horseradish in a thin layer. On another section of the same sheet, spread out the lime zest. On yet another section of the sheet, make a pile of 1 tsp of the fine sea salt. Make a well in the center of the pile, gently pour the Worcestershire into the well, and mix it with the salt to keep it from spreading. **Dry at 135°F [57°C] for 14 to 18 hours**, until the shallot and tomato slices are brittle, the horseradish crumbles when pinched, and the Worcestershire salt is dry to the touch. Let cool completely.

3. Break the tomato slices into small pieces. In a spice grinder, working in three or four batches, pulverize the tomatoes, shallot, horseradish, Worcestershire salt, and lime zest into a fine powder, adding some of the remaining fine sea salt to each batch to help prevent sticking. (To prevent the grinder from jamming, start grinding with the grinder upside down and then turn it right-side up.) Place the powdered ingredients into a small bowl. Add the sugar, black pepper, celery seeds, cayenne, and flaky sea salt and stir to combine.

4. Store in an airtight container, preferably with a silica gel packet to extend freshness, in a dark place at room temperature for up to 3 months.

Lavender is a tricky ingredient. A tiny dusting, like in Humboldt Fog's Purple Haze goat cheese, and you've got the perfect whiff of summer in your cheese course—all sunbaked meadows and warm mountain breezes. On the other hand, I've had a few lavender ice creams that have made me feel like I was eating the soap from the guest bathroom. In this herb salt recipe, I use just a tiny bit of lavender flowers—providing only an undertone, really—in a dried seasoning mixture that's perfect for roast meats. Lavender isn't necessary to a Provençal herb mix, but I think you'll find it irresistible.

HERBES DE PROVENCE SALT

MAKES ABOUT ⅓ CUP [50 G]

20 sprigs fresh oregano

20 sprigs fresh thyme

10 to 12 sprigs fresh lavender with flowers

One 6-in [15-cm] sprig fresh rosemary

3 Tbsp fine sea salt

1. Line dehydrator trays with non-stick mesh sheets that have been lightly coated with cooking oil.

2. Lay out the oregano, thyme, lavender, and rosemary sprigs on the prepared trays. **Dry at 125°F [52°C] for 4 to 6 hours**, until dry and brittle. Let cool completely.

3. Pluck the blossoms off the lavender stems and pull the leaves off the oregano, thyme, and rosemary stems. In a medium bowl, mix together the lavender blossoms and herb leaves.

4. In a spice grinder, working in batches, pulse the herb mixture about five times, pulverizing it into a coarse powder. Add the salt and pulse once more to mix.

5. Store in an airtight container, preferably with a silica gel packet to extend freshness, in a dark place at room temperature for up to 6 months.

There's no better fit for the warm-earth aromas of Herbes de Provence Salt than lamb, simply grilled. The combination is summertime in a meal.

RACK OF LAMB WITH HERBES DE PROVENCE SALT

SERVES 6 TO 8

Two 8-chop lamb racks (1¼ to 1½ lb [570 to 680 g])

1 Tbsp olive oil

1 garlic clove, peeled and minced

1 anchovy fillet, rinsed and minced

1 Tbsp Herbes de Provence Salt (page 33)

⅛ tsp freshly ground black pepper

Flaky sea salt

Fresh thyme leaves for garnish (optional)

1. At least 30 minutes (or up to 1 day) before cooking, trim the lamb chops of any excess flesh between the bones and any thick layers of fat along the meat. Separate the chops by slicing between each bone. (You can have the butcher "French" and separate the chops for you, if you prefer.)

2. In a small bowl, stir together the olive oil, garlic, and anchovy. Rub the oil mixture all over the fleshy part of the lamb chops. In a small bowl, stir together the herbes de Provence salt and black pepper. Dust the fleshy parts of the chops with the seasoning mixture and rub it in for even coating.

3. If the meat is chilled, remove it from the refrigerator at least a half hour before cooking. Preheat a gas grill to high; preheat a charcoal grill to hot; preheat coals if cooking on charcoal; or if you plan to use the oven, place the oven rack just below the broiler and have a sturdy baking sheet available.

4. Cook the chops on the grill or under the broiler to the desired doneness, which will vary with the size of the chops: small lamb chops (like those from Australia and New Zealand) will take about 3 minutes on each side for medium-rare. Arrange the cooked chops on a platter and lightly sprinkle with sea salt and thyme, if desired. Serve immediately.

Old-fashioned, richly scented roses work best for this flavor booster, which lends a mysterious lilt to shortbread, yogurt, iced tea, or the whipped cream you dollop on a summer pie. I have an absurdly productive mauve rosebush in my backyard, and I've been harvesting its blooms for the kitchen instead of for bouquets. The resulting sweet powder is lilac in color and lightly fragrant. Just be sure the roses you are sourcing have not been treated with insecticide.

ROSE SUGAR

MAKES ABOUT ⅔ CUP [60 G]

4 cups [90 g] fresh organic rose petals

¼ cup [50 g] sugar

1. Line dehydrator trays with nonstick mesh sheets. (No need to oil.)

2. Pick over the rose petals and discard any leaves, unsightly petals, or bugs.

3. Lay out the petals in single layers on the prepared trays. **Dry at 125°F [52°C] for 36 to 48 hours**, until completely dry and crisp. Let cool completely.

4. In a spice grinder, working in batches, pulverize the dried rose petals with 2 Tbsp of the sugar into a fine powder. Pour into a bowl. Stir the rose sugar together with the remaining sugar.

5. Store in an airtight container, preferably with a silica gel packet to extend freshness, in a dark place at room temperature for up to 6 months.

Persian cooking uses the brilliant combination of rose with cardamom in a lot of desserts—it's a softly evocative way to make something as simple as a shortbread cookie linger on the palate. I love these cookies with afternoon tea, or broken into shards sprinkled over vanilla ice cream.

ROSE-CARDAMOM SHORTBREAD

MAKES 32 BARS

2 cups [240 g] all-purpose flour

1⅓ cups [120 g] oat flour

1 tsp salt

¾ tsp ground cardamom

1⅓ cups [290 g] unsalted butter, at room temperature

¾ cup [150 g] granulated sugar

2 Tbsp Rose Sugar (page 36)

1 tsp rose water

1. Preheat the oven to 275°F [135°C]. Butter a 9-by-13-in [23-by-33-cm] baking pan, and line the bottom with parchment paper.

2. In a large bowl, whisk together the all-purpose flour, oat flour, salt, and cardamom. Set aside.

3. Combine the butter, granulated sugar, and rose sugar in the bowl of an electric mixer fitted with the paddle attachment (or in a medium bowl with a handheld mixer). Beat on medium speed until creamy and light, about 2 minutes. Mix in the rose water. With the mixer on low speed, gradually add the flour mixture, 1 cup [115 g] at a time, and beat just until combined.

4. Press the dough into the prepared pan; a clean drinking glass works well for pressing the mixture into the corners and smoothing the surface. Using a butter knife or a bench knife, cut down through the dough lengthwise to make eight even strips. Cut down through the dough crosswise to make four even strips, making a total of thirty-two bars. Prick the surface of the dough with the tines of a fork.

5. Bake until evenly pale golden but not browned, 80 to 90 minutes. Remove the pan to a wire rack and let cool for about 15 minutes.

6. Flip the pan to release the shortbread onto a cutting board, and remove the parchment. Carefully break the shortbread into bars along the cut lines (you can also cut the warm bars again with a sharp knife if the incisions have not held during baking). Let cool completely.

7. Store in an airtight container at room temperature for up to 1 month.

There is nothing like the bright intensity of this marigold-colored sugar to add interest to a sugar cookie or enliven your favorite muffin recipe. You can even use it as an easy way to add intrigue to your iced tea—stir into hot, double-steeped tea before pouring over ice. To gather the orange and lemon zest, I like to use a sharp Y-shaped potato peeler to remove only the brightly colored peel in strips, leaving the white pith behind. Since it's easy to dry citrus peel, I always do a little more than I need for the sugar. Later on, I'll add a small strip of peel to a stew or soup; I'm always surprised at the fragrance and depth it imparts.

CITRUS SUGAR

MAKES ABOUT 1¼ CUPS [115 G]

**Zest strips from
3 navel oranges**

Zest strips from 2 lemons

¾ cup [150 g] sugar

1. Lay out the orange and lemon zest strips on dehydrator trays. (There's no need to line the trays, because the strips are big enough to not fall through standard tray holes, and they're not sticky.) **Dry at 135°F [57°C] for 8 to 12 hours,** until dry and crisp. Let cool completely.

2. Break the zest into small pieces. (You can do this easily by placing the zest in a ziptop bag and then pounding and rolling it with a rolling pin.)

3. In a spice grinder, working in batches, pulverize the zest with about two-thirds of the sugar into a very fine powder with some small bits of peel in it. (To prevent the grinder from jamming, start grinding with the grinder upside down and then turn it right-side up.) Sift the sugar-zest powder to remove any remaining particles of zest. Stir in the remaining sugar.

4. Store in an airtight container, preferably with a silica gel packet to extend freshness, in a dark place at room temperature for up to 6 months.

I used to be a huge fan of Japanese panko crumbs, but now I'm inclined to use my own flavorful bread crumbs. The dehydrator lets you use your aging bread to make incredibly fluffy, crisp crumbs to top broiled seafood, tenderize meatballs, and enrobe chicken or fish fillets. You can use almost any bread to make delicious crumbs, but white bread crumbs keep longer than dark-flour bread crumbs. Put rye or whole-wheat crumbs into the freezer for long-term storage.

SEASONED BREAD CRUMBS

MAKES ABOUT 4 CUPS [360 G]

2 sprigs fresh oregano

1½ lb [680 g] white sourdough bread, sliced

1 Tbsp fine sea salt

½ tsp freshly ground black pepper

¼ tsp cayenne pepper

1. Line dehydrator trays with non-stick mesh sheets that have been lightly coated with cooking oil.

2. Place the oregano on the bottom prepared tray. Lay out the bread slices on the remaining prepared trays. **Dry at 160°F [71°C] for 3 to 4 hours**, until the bread is crackly dry. Let cool completely.

3. Break the bread into chunks, place as much as you can into the bowl of a food processor (or blender), and pulse until reduced to coarse crumbs. Add the remaining bread and process into very fine, even crumbs, about 2 minutes.

4. Remove the stems from the dried oregano and discard. Add the leaves to the bread crumbs, along with the salt, black pepper, and cayenne. Pulse until well combined.

5. Store in an airtight container, preferably with a silica gel packet to extend freshness, in a dark place at room temperature for up to 1 week, or in the freezer for up to 6 months.

This is the kind of dish I sometimes make for the kids when I'm serving something spicier or more complicated to my adult dinner guests. Then all the adults look at me balefully because they want to be eating breaded chicken, too.

CHICKEN WITH PARMESAN CRUST

SERVES 4

Canola oil for drizzling

2 boneless, skinless chicken breasts, split

Fine sea salt

Freshly ground black pepper

1 cup [120 g] all-purpose flour

2 eggs, lightly beaten with 2 Tbsp water

1½ cups [135 g] Seasoned Bread Crumbs (facing page)

⅓ cup [45 g] freshly grated Parmigiano-Reggiano cheese

4 Tbsp [55 g] clarified butter

Lemon wedges for garnish

1. Drizzle a bit of canola oil on a sheet of plastic wrap. If any of the chicken breasts still have their tenders—the thin strip on the underside of the breast—pull them off and set aside. Lay one chicken breast piece on the plastic wrap and drizzle it with a bit more canola oil. Top with another sheet of plastic wrap. Using the smooth side of a meat mallet or a wooden rolling pin, pound the chicken until it is even and about ½ in [12 mm] thick. Repeat with the three remaining breast pieces. Season the chicken breasts and tenders lightly with salt and pepper.

2. In a shallow bowl, put half of the flour. In a second shallow bowl, add the beaten egg. In a third shallow bowl, mix together about half the seasoned bread crumbs with half the Parmigiano-Reggiano cheese. Dip one chicken piece into the flour and dust thoroughly on all sides. Using one hand, dip the piece into the egg, and turn to coat completely. Using the same hand, dip the piece into the bread crumbs, and coat completely. Place on a plate, and repeat with the remaining pieces and the tenders. Refresh the bowls with the remaining flour and bread crumbs as needed. Set a wire rack atop a baking sheet.

3. In a large, deep skillet over medium heat, warm 2 Tbsp of the clarified butter. Drop a few bread crumbs into the hot oil; when they sizzle vigorously, the pan is ready for the chicken (if the oil is smoking, it is too hot, so adjust the heat). Put two chicken breast pieces into the hot oil, and cook until the bread crumbs are a light almond brown, 3 to 4 minutes. Turn the chicken pieces and cook for another 3 to 4 minutes, until they are done. You can use a small knife to check; when the chicken is just opaque, it is done. Remove the chicken pieces to the prepared rack.

4. Pour off the hot butter from the skillet into a small heatproof vessel and add the remaining 2 Tbsp clarified butter to the pan. Cook the remaining chicken in the same manner.

5. Serve the chicken with lemon wedges.

Dried shrimp are one of the most striking dried food discoveries I have made. I use the tasty bay shrimp from nearby Oregon waters that fill our markets in the fall. When dried, they add incredible depth to any dish they garnish, from eggs to Southeast Asian salads to grits. I even cadged a recipe for devastating chile-shrimp jam (see page 44), a funky-sweet-salty condiment of kings, from my friends PK and Wiley Frank at Little Uncle, my favorite Seattle Thai restaurant. Be warned, however. Along with garlic, shrimp is among the smelliest ingredients you can dry. If you can, dry it in the garage or basement, where it won't bum out your housemates.

DRIED SHRIMP

MAKES ABOUT 1 CUP [80 G]

2 lb [910 g] peeled cooked bay shrimp

1. Line dehydrator trays with non-stick mesh sheets that have been lightly coated with cooking oil.

2. Spread the shrimp on the prepared trays. **Dry at 160°F [71°C] for 8 to 12 hours**, until dry and crackly. Let cool completely.

3. Store in an airtight container, preferably with a silica gel packet to extend freshness, in a dark place at room temperature for up to 1 week, or in the freezer for up to 6 months.

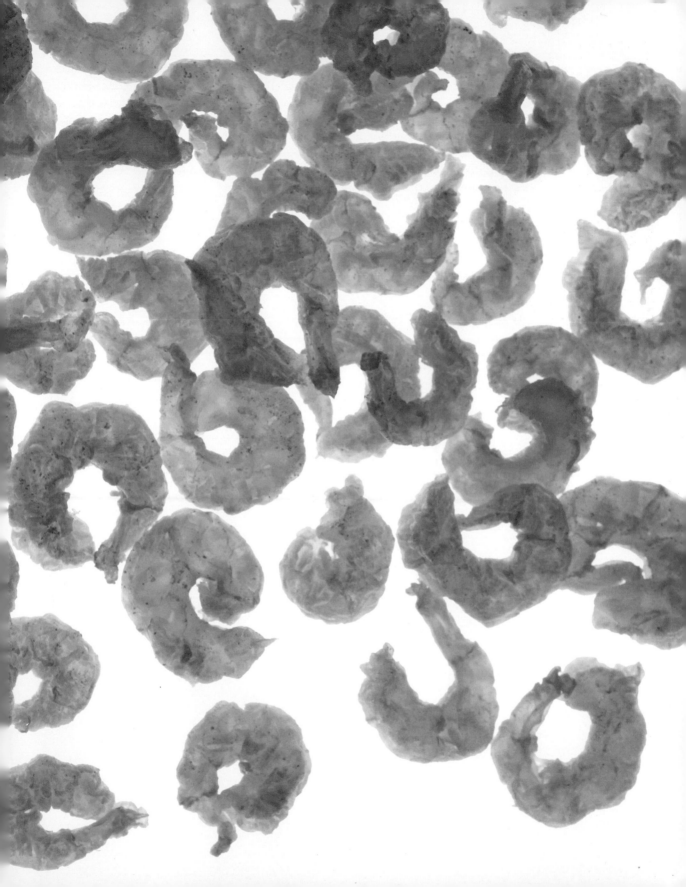

This Thai condiment, called *nam prik pao*, makes everything sing, from barbecued ribs and stir-fried greens to white toast. It's a bit of work, but well worth it if you like big flavor. If you do not have a large, solid mortar and pestle, you can use a food processor (or blender) to grind the ingredients in succession, but the finished product will be a bit grittier. Make this recipe with your windows open and the vent fan turned on if you have one, since the cooking chiles can cause you to tear up or cough. The first step of the recipe calls for making a juice out of tamarind paste, which can be found at Asian markets. This step can be done up to a week in advance, and the recipe makes a bit more tamarind juice than necessary. Any leftover tamarind juice can be stirred into a curry or mixed with club soda and honey for a tangy drink.

LITTLE UNCLE'S CHILE SHRIMP JAM

MAKES 3½ CUPS [600 ML]

¼ cup [60 g] tamarind paste

1¾ cups [420 ml] water

3 cups [720 ml] vegetable oil

2 cups [190 g] thinly sliced shallots

1 cup [90 g] smashed or thinly sliced garlic cloves

½ cup [45 g] Dried Shrimp (page 42)

5 dried Thai chiles, whole, stemmed

½ cup [60 g] smashed or thinly sliced palm sugar

1½ Tbsp kosher salt

1. In a small, nonreactive saucepan, combine the tamarind paste and water. Bring to a boil, breaking up the paste with the end of a whisk or a potato masher. Turn off the heat, cover, and let steep for 30 minutes. Strain into a bowl, pressing firmly to get as much liquid and pulp through the strainer as possible. Scrape the exterior of the strainer into the liquid and discard the solids. Measure 1 cup [240 ml] of the strained tamarind juice. Any excess can be stored in a sealed jar in the refrigerator for up to 1 week for another use.

2. In a medium wok or heavy, deep saucepan, heat the vegetable oil to 350°F [180°C]

3. Put a plate next to the wok for a landing spot, and have a spider or slotted spoon ready.

4. Add the shallots to the oil and fry until very light golden brown, 5 to 8 minutes. With the spider, remove the shallots to the plate. The shallots will continue to cook out of the oil, so do not overcook or they will be bitter. Add the garlic to the oil and fry until golden brown, 1 to 2 minutes, then remove to the plate.

5. Add the dried shrimp to the oil and fry until they darken, 2 to 4 minutes. Let the shrimp cool a bit and try one. The shrimp should be brittle, not chewy, but also not burnt and bitter. Transfer to the plate.

6. Hold your breath. Add the chiles to the oil and fry briefly until they get a shade darker. Remove to the plate. Turn off the heat under the wok.

7. With a mortar and pestle, progressively smash the fried ingredients. Start with the shrimp, and smash until they have a sandy appearance. Add the shallots, and smash until they also have a sandy appearance. Add the garlic, and smash. Add the chiles, and smash.

8. Put the smashed mixture into a medium saucepan over low heat. Add the strained tamarind juice, palm sugar, and salt. Bring to a simmer and cook, stirring often to dissolve the palm sugar, until it has a jam-like consistency. The jam will thicken when cooled. Taste the jam; it should be savory (garlic/shallot/shrimp), slightly sweet (palm sugar), slightly tangy (tamarind), salty (salt), and spicy (chiles). Remove from the heat and let cool.

9. Store in an airtight container in the refrigerator for up to 1 month.

CHAPTER 2:
ALTERED
FRUIT

As a youngster, my brother was a famously insatiable dried-fruit eater. His appetite for tangy sweet dried apricots and sour cherries stunned my parents and their friends whose pantries he raided. Even today, he calls me with hot tips on the best dried fruit (dried tangerines are a new fixation). He was right to be obsessed; the dehydrator is a great friend to fruit.

If you want to try out the potential of your dehydrator, make your own raisins. Choose the best grapes you can get your hands on (seedless are definitely easier), preferably something from your late-summer farmers' market. Drop the stemmed grapes in boiling water for a couple of minutes, just until their skins split, and then drain. Lay them out on a dehydrator tray and dry in the dehydrator until, well, raisin-y. The skin will be wrinkly, the interior flesh chewy-soft. With green grapes, you'll get a vibrantly tart result, while red and black grapes yield something decidedly earthier and sweeter. No matter which type, the raisins will have more personality than store-bought varieties. You'll find yourself serving them not just on cereal, but alongside cheese, on salads, and by the handful on their own.

Some fruits do really well with minimal processing before drying, and some are made even better with a little manipulation before they hit the dehydrator—hence the concept of "altered fruit." A little tweak here or there can make delicious fruit even more intriguing. Unsweetened dried cranberries are painfully bitter, so I macerate them overnight in orange juice before drying them to tangy sweet perfection. Some fruits aren't well served by drying on their own. Blueberries and blackberries, for instance, lose their lush juiciness and end up a little tough. I prefer to blend them with other fruits in a fruit leather, where their color and flavor really shine.

Other fruits just invite experimentation. You can make your dried plums more aromatic by soaking them in Earl Grey tea after drying them, or letting cherries linger in vermouth before drying. After you've got your boozy cherry, you can use the flavored vermouth and the dried cherry in a signature Manhattan.

Perhaps the trickiest aspect of getting dried fruit the way you like it is controlling the texture. Some pieces of fruit may dry more quickly and fully than others. While not essential, the process of conditioning—agitating dried fruit daily for several days before packaging for long-term storage (see page 21)—can help even out texture within a batch of fruit, and also manage the remaining moisture so that the fruit lasts longer in storage.

On hiking trips, dried sour cherries keep my family moving forward over hills, rocks, and streams. At the farmers' market, when I see fresh sour (or "pie") cherries during their brief season, I pounce on them for dehydrating. If you dry them untreated, they are a wonderful souring ingredient in stews, but they're not quite snacking material. In this recipe, I dry them first and then soak them in a syrup sweetened just lightly with agave syrup. I drain them and dry them again briefly, so they're ready to go into the next batch of whole-grain salad, double-chocolate cookie dough, or a take-along bag for climbing a mountain. If you cannot find fresh sour cherries, see if your grocery can get frozen unsweetened sour cherries. If so, just thaw in the refrigerator and drain them before drying.

AGAVE-KISSED SOUR CHERRIES

MAKES ABOUT ¾ CUP [75 G]

2 lb [910 g] fresh sour cherries, stemmed

½ cup [120 ml] water

2 Tbsp agave syrup

1 tsp balsamic vinegar

1. Line dehydrator trays with non-stick mesh sheets that have been lightly coated with cooking oil.

2. Pit the cherries. Lay them out in a single layer on the prepared trays. **Dry at 135°F [57°C] for 22 to 26 hours,** until they are wrinkled and don't feel squishy when pinched.

3. In a medium nonreactive saucepan over high heat, bring the water, agave syrup, and balsamic vinegar to a boil. Add the dried cherries, stir, and turn the heat to low. Simmer for 2 to 3 minutes. Remove from the heat and let the cherries stand in the syrup for about 20 minutes, then drain.

4. Meanwhile, wash and dry the dehydrator trays and line them with mesh sheets that have been lightly coated with cooking oil.

5. Lay out the cherries on the prepared trays. **Dry at 135°F [57°C] for 1 hour,** until dry to the touch. Let cool completely. You may choose to condition the dried cherries at this point (see page 21).

6. Store in an airtight container, preferably with a silica gel packet to extend freshness, in a dark place at room temperature for up to 1 month, in the refrigerator for up to 2 months, or in the freezer for up to 1 year.

What I love about scones is the way the crispy edges converse with the soft, tender interior, something that can be dismayingly hard to find outside a home kitchen. The scones in coffeehouses tend to be steroidally oversized, sort of shapeless, and endlessly bland. These are small simple scones with a bit of tartness from yogurt to echo the sweet-tart glory of dried sour cherries. For an extra citrus kick, sprinkle the scones with more Citrus Sugar in place of the Demerara sugar. Eat two if you're hungry; you'll have even more corners to nibble. This is a smallish batch, since scones aren't meant for keeping a long time. Double up the recipe if you're having a crowd.

DRIED CHERRY CREAM SCONES

MAKES 8 SMALL SCONES

2 cups [240 g] all-purpose flour

4 Tbsp [50 g] Citrus Sugar (page 39) or granulated sugar

2 tsp baking powder

1 tsp baking soda

¾ tsp salt

5 Tbsp [70 g] cold butter, cut into ½-in [12-mm] pieces

½ cup [50 g] dried Agave-Kissed Sour Cherries (facing page), coarsely chopped

⅓ cup [80 ml] whole-milk yogurt

⅓ cup [80 ml] cream, plus 2 Tbsp

2 eggs

2 tsp grated orange zest (if using granulated sugar)

1 Tbsp Demerara sugar or granulated sugar

1. Preheat the oven to 400°F [200°C]. Line a baking sheet with parchment paper or a silicone baking mat.

2. In a large bowl, whisk together the flour, citrus sugar, baking powder, baking soda, and salt. Add the butter pieces to the flour mixture and toss to coat. Using cool fingers, rub the butter into the flour mixture until the combination is mostly sandy in texture with a few pea-size lumps of flour-coated butter. Add the dried cherries and stir to distribute evenly.

3. In a small bowl or liquid measuring cup, thoroughly whisk together the yogurt and ⅓ cup [80 ml] cream, one of the eggs, and the orange zest (if using). Make a well in the flour mixture and pour in the cream mixture. Stir until just combined to form a damp, sticky paste. Using lightly floured hands, pull together the dough into a rough ball.

4. On a lightly floured work surface, pat the dough into a roughly circular mass about 6 in [15 cm] wide and 1½ in [4 cm] thick. Using a bench scraper or butter knife, cut the dough into eight even wedges (or into six wedges, if you like a bigger scone). Put the wedges onto the prepared baking sheet, leaving about 2 in [5 cm] between the scones.

5. In the small bowl, whisk together the remaining egg with the 2 Tbsp cream to make an egg wash. Brush the top of each scone evenly with the egg wash. Sprinkle each scone with a bit of the Demerara sugar.

6. Bake for 20 to 25 minutes, until the tops of the scones are golden brown. Serve warm or room temperature.

Manhattans are a delicious cocktail, but their cherries sometimes disappoint. In my first foray into creative dehydrating (as part of an article I did for Slate), I had the idea to soak the cherry in vermouth, the key aromatic element of a Manhattan, and then dry it to a pleasantly chewy texture. The leftover soaking liquid could go into the cocktail, pushing the cherry flavor forward. Mixed together with the whiskey, these elements added compelling nuance to the classic cocktail.

VERMOUTH DRIED CHERRIES

MAKES ABOUT ¾ CUP [90 G]

1½ lb [680 g] fresh sweet cherries, like Bing or Lambert, stemmed

2 cups [480 ml] red vermouth (like Martini & Rossi)

1. Pit the cherries. Combine them with the vermouth in a baking dish. Let soak for 8 hours, or overnight, stirring once or twice.

2. Line dehydrator trays with non-stick mesh sheets that have been lightly coated with cooking oil.

3. Drain the cherries (pour the soaking liquid into a sterilized jar and reserve for cocktail making; it will keep for several months at room temperature). Lay them out on the prepared trays. **Dry at 135°F [57°C] for 24 hours**, or until they are no longer squishy but pleasantly chewy. Let cool completely. You may choose to condition the dried cherries at this point (see page 21).

4. Store in an airtight container, preferably with a silica gel packet to extend freshness, in a dark place at room temperature for up to 1 month, in the refrigerator for up to 2 months, or in the freezer for up to 1 year.

Here's a classic rye Manhattan where the cherry flavor is turned up a bit thanks to the cherry-infused vermouth left over from soaking the fruit. Because the drink is fruit-forward, don't choose a sweet bourbon like Maker's Mark for this drink, but stick with a sterner whiskey like 1776 or Bulleit rye.

THE DRIED CHERRY MANHATTAN

SERVES 1

Cracked ice

2 oz [60 ml] rye whiskey

1 oz [30 ml] cherry-infused vermouth (see Vermouth Dried Cherries, page 50)

2 dashes of bitters, Angostura for traditional flavor or Xocolatl Mole–flavored bitters for a hint of spice

1 Vermouth Dried Cherry (page 50)

Fill a pitcher with cracked ice. Add the rye, vermouth, and bitters and stir to mix. Strain into a chilled cocktail glass and garnish with the dried cherry. Serve immediately

Cranberries, though richly flavored, need a little help. They have tough skins, and they are too bitter to enjoy out of hand when they are dried on their own. Here, I cook them just briefly to pop their skins and let them soak in a sweetened orange juice. They then dry up sweet-tart and perfect for baking and for gobbling straight. (They are still less sweet than the sugary dried cranberries you find at the grocery.) As a bonus by-product, the soaking liquid can be used to make a pretty pink spritzer—either nonalcoholic with sparkling water, or with Champagne. You also can freeze the soaking liquid and use it again for another batch of cranberries.

DRIED ORANGE CRANBERRIES

MAKES ABOUT 1 PT [100 G]

3 cups [720 ml] fresh orange juice

2 cups [400 g] sugar

2 pt [400 g] cranberries, rinsed and picked over

1. In a large nonreactive saucepan over medium-high heat, combine the orange juice and sugar. Stir until the sugar is dissolved. Add the cranberries, bring to a boil, then turn the heat to low and simmer for a few minutes until you hear the cranberries popping. Stir for 1 to 2 minutes, until most of the cranberries' skins have split. Let cool, then refrigerate the cranberries in the liquid overnight. Drain the cranberries, reserving the liquid if you like.

2. Line dehydrator trays with non-stick mesh sheets that have been lightly coated with cooking oil.

3. Lay out the cranberries, separated from one another, on the prepared trays. **Dry at 135°F [57°C] for 20 to 24 hours,** until they are somewhat leathery on the outside and no longer puffy-soft in the center. Stir the cranberries and rotate the trays a few times during the drying process, and make sure to separate any berries that have clumped together. Let cool completely. You may choose to condition the cranberries at this point (see page 21).

4. Store in an airtight container, preferably with a silica gel packet to extend freshness, in a dark place at room temperature for up to 3 months, or in the freezer for up to 1 year.

Tisane is a pretty word for herbal tea. (It's also more accurate, since there's no tea in a tisane!) If you've got an herb garden, your dehydrator can keep you stocked with soothing drinks well beyond the green months. In this recipe, I've combined the honeyed fragrance of chamomile with some crisp mint and lemon verbena, plus the tang of raspberries, which lend a sweet blush tone. If you don't have access to some of the fresh ingredients, or if you have dried them in bulk beforehand, I have given measurements for dried ingredients in the blend as well. Chamomile flowers, peppermint, and verbena are also commonly available in health food or tea stores. To steep, use 1 Tbsp tisane per 1 cup [240 ml] boiling water. Brew for 4 to 5 minutes, and serve with honey or sugar. You can also substitute fresh lemon zest strips for the verbena. Dry the strips along with the raspberries. Chop the zest strips into small pieces and blend with the tea.

RASPBERRY CHAMOMILE TISANE

MAKES ABOUT 1½ CUPS [30 G]

1 pt [170 g] raspberries

2 cups [40 g] organic chamomile flowers, or ½ cup [15 g] dried chamomile flowers

12 sprigs fresh mint, or ½ cup [8 g] loosely packed dried mint leaves

5 sprigs fresh lemon verbena, or ¼ cup [2 g] loosely packed dried lemon verbena leaves

1. Line dehydrator trays with nonstick mesh sheets that have been lightly coated with cooking oil. Also have ready a few extra trays lined with ungreased nonstick mesh sheets.

2. Place the berries on the prepared trays. **Dry at 135°F [57°C] for 18 to 24 hours**, until the berries are dry enough to crumble when pinched. Let cool completely.

3. Place the chamomile flowers, mint sprigs, and lemon verbena sprigs on the ungreased sheets. **Dry at 125°F [52°C] for 4 to 6 hours**, until dry and crumbly. Let cool completely.

4. Remove the mint and verbena leaves from the stems and crumble into fragments into a small bowl. Add the dried raspberries and chamomile and stir to combine.

5. Store in an airtight container, preferably with a silica gel packet to extend freshness, in a dark place at room temperature for up to 6 months.

I served these grapes at a holiday dinner just as the Seattle days were at their shortest. Full of sweet spice and the evocative, almost medieval complexity of port, these syrup-soaked raisins are just the thing to offer with an aged chunk of Cheddar or a slab of delicious country pâté. For added visual effect, you could keep the grapes on their stems.

PORT WINE GRAPES

MAKES ABOUT ⅔ CUP [75 G]

1½ lb [680 g] seedless red grapes

2 cups [480 ml] port

1 star anise

1 cinnamon stick

One 3-in [7.5-cm] strip orange zest

1. In a medium, nonreactive saucepan over medium-high heat, combine the grapes, port, star anise, cinnamon stick, and orange zest. (The port should reach the top of the grapes; if not, add a bit of water.) Bring to a boil, then turn the heat to low and simmer for 4 to 6 minutes, until the grape skins develop small fissures. Let cool completely.

2. Line dehydrator trays with non-stick mesh sheets that have been lightly coated with cooking oil.

3. Strain the grapes, reserving the port and discarding the other solids. Lay out the grapes on the prepared trays. **Dry at 135°F [57°C] for 16 to 24 hours,** until the grapes are wrinkled and no longer squishy to the touch. Let cool completely.

4. Bring the port liquid to a boil over medium-high heat, then turn the heat to low and simmer, stirring frequently, until the reduced syrup coats the back of a spoon. Let cool, then stir in the dried grapes.

5. Store in an airtight container in the refrigerator for up to 1 month.

I have a weakness for yogurt-coated pretzels, cranberries, and raisins from the bulk section at the grocery store, though I think there is very little yogurt in those. In trying to devise my own more natural yogurt coating, I worked my way through various methods (gelatin, confectioners' sugar) but was unsatisfied until I tried a clingy coating of Greek yogurt, coconut oil (which is solid at room temperature), and white chocolate. Just make sure to let the mixture harden at a cool room temperature for at least a day before packing for storage.

YOGURT-COATED RAISINS

MAKES ABOUT 4 CUPS [610 G]

2 lb [910 g] seedless black grapes

¾ cup [135 g] white chocolate chips

¼ cup [60 g] nonfat Greek yogurt

1 Tbsp coconut oil

1. Line dehydrator trays with nonstick mesh sheets that have been lightly coated with cooking oil.

2. Bring a pot of water to a boil over medium-high heat. Immerse the grapes, turn the heat to low, and simmer for 2 to 4 minutes, until the grape skins crack. With a slotted spoon, remove the grapes to a plate. Let cool completely.

3. Lay out the grapes on the prepared trays. **Dry at 135°F [57°C] for 16 to 20 hours,** until the grapes are chewy, not squishy, through to their centers. Grape size will influence drying, so check frequently. Let cool completely.

4. Lay a fine-mesh dehydrator sheet atop a wire cooling rack, and put over a baking sheet.

5. Put the chocolate chips in a medium microwave-safe bowl. Melt the chips in the microwave in 30-second intervals, stirring after each interval, until smooth. Whisk the yogurt and coconut oil into the white chocolate, stirring until smooth. Put the raisins in the yogurt-chocolate mixture, and stir to coat well.

6. Spread the coated raisins on the prepared rack. Let sit overnight, while the coating firms up.

7. Store in an airtight container, preferably with a silica gel packet to extend freshness, in a dark place at room temperature for up to 2 weeks, or in the freezer for up to 6 months.

Here is the basic chewy kind of dried apple I grew up with, but it's given an apple-pie treatment with a bit of sugar and cinnamon. While these are tasty to nibble on their own, I really love them stirred into hot morning breakfasts (see page 146) and baked goods. They're particularly good mixed with fresh fruit in a pie or cobbler; the dried apples will soak up some of the fresh fruit juices and help prevent a soggy crust.

DRIED CINNAMON APPLES

MAKES ABOUT 1¾ CUPS [35 G]

2 lb [910 g] tart apples (such as Granny Smith or Braeburn), peeled, cored, and cut into ⅓-in- [8-mm-] thick slices

2 Tbsp fresh lemon juice

1 Tbsp sugar

½ tsp cinnamon

Pinch of salt

1. Line dehydrator trays with non-stick mesh sheets that have been lightly coated with cooking oil.

2. In a large bowl, combine the apple slices and lemon juice and toss to coat well. Sprinkle in the sugar, cinnamon, and salt and toss to coat thoroughly.

3. Lay out the apple slices on the prepared trays. **Dry at 135°F [57°C] for 6 to 8 hours**, until they are dry, springy, and still pliable. Flip the apples and rotate the trays at least once during the drying process. Let cool completely. You may choose to condition the apples at this point (see page 21).

4. Store in an airtight container, preferably with a silica gel packet to extend freshness, in a dark place at room temperature for up to 3 months, or in the freezer for up to 1 year.

I grew up enjoying thick-cut dried apple slices that had a distinctive sponginess. They were tasty, but once I discovered the pleasures of snacking on paper-thin crispy slices of apple, I was a convert. If you're feeding kids or other fussy eaters, you may want to core the apples before drying. Otherwise, these are especially beautiful cut lengthwise, core and all. As is the case with other crispy-dried ingredients, these chips will stay edible for a long time, but their texture will be at its most pleasing snappiest within a few days of drying. They can be refreshed by placing them back in the dehydrator for 1 to 2 hours.

APPLE CHIPS

MAKES ABOUT 1 CUP [20 G]

1 qt [960 ml] water

1 tsp citric acid

1 lb [455 g] apples, cored, if desired, and sliced crosswise less than 1/8 in [3 mm] thick

1. Line dehydrator trays with non-stick mesh sheets that have been lightly coated with cooking oil.

2. In a large bowl, combine the water and citric acid and stir well to dissolve. Submerge the apple slices in the solution, turning them gently to make sure each apple slice is coated, and then drain.

3. Lay out the apple slices on the prepared trays. (If you are working with a box dehydrator, and you have spare mesh tray liners, you can lay one atop each apple-filled tray to minimize the curling of the apple slices as they dry.) **Dry at 135°F [57°C] for 4 to 6 hours**, until completely dry and crisp. Let cool completely.

4. Store in an airtight container, preferably with a silica gel packet to extend freshness, in a dark place at room temperature for up to 1 month.

I really love pears, but they taste a little drab when dried on their own. When dried after being poached in a light lemon-vanilla syrup, on the other hand, you get sweet cross sections to serve alongside cheese or as an audacious garnish for, say, salted caramel ice cream. This is another recipe where a mandoline can help you to cut very thin, uniform slices. The thinner the slices, the crisper the texture. Slightly thicker slices are good too, but they will yield a chewy fruit-leather-like mouthfeel.

SWEET VANILLA PEAR SLICES

MAKES ABOUT 3½ CUPS [135 G]

4 cups [960 ml] water

1 cup [200 g] sugar

2 Tbsp cider vinegar

1 lemon, cut into ¼-in- [6-mm-] thick slices

1 Tbsp vanilla extract

4 pears, cut lengthwise into slices less than ⅛ in [3 mm] thick

1. Line dehydrator trays with non-stick mesh sheets that have been lightly coated with cooking oil.

2. In a large, wide, nonreactive saucepan over high heat, bring the water, sugar, vinegar, lemon slices, and vanilla to a boil. Turn the heat to low, and simmer. Carefully slip the pear slices into the hot syrup, and press gently down with a spoon to make sure they are immersed. Simmer for 10 minutes, until the slices are translucent but still hold together well.

3. Drain the pears, reserving the syrup to sweeten tea or for future batches, if desired.

4. Lay out the pear slices on the prepared trays. **Dry at 135°F [57°C] for 6 to 8 hours,** until crisp. You can stop the drying process earlier, when the slices are more leathery, which can also be a nice effect. Let cool completely. You may choose to condition the pears at this point (see page 21).

5. Store in an airtight container, preferably with a silica gel packet to extend freshness, in a dark place at room temperature for up to 3 months, or in the freezer for up to 1 year.

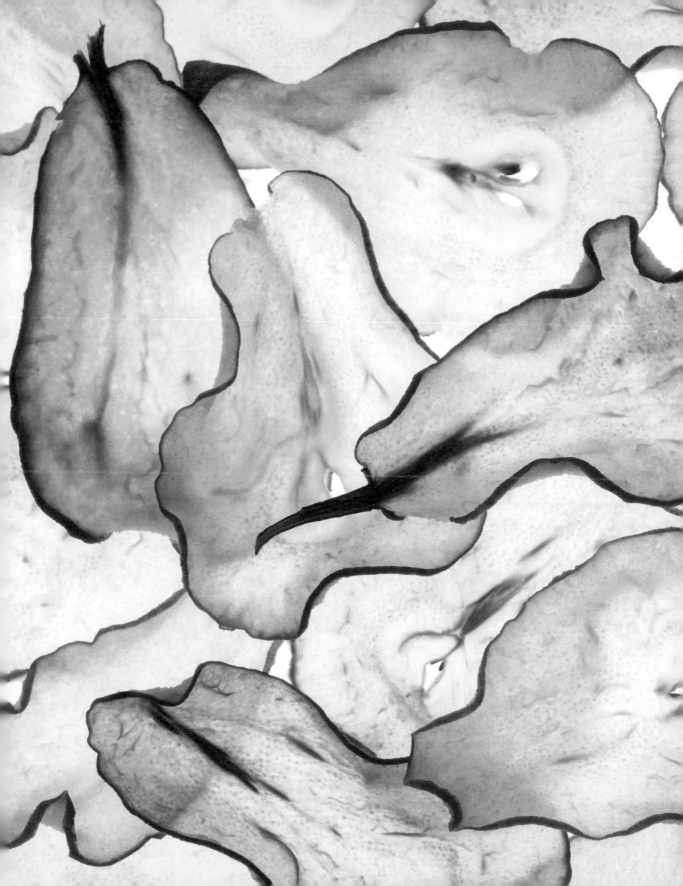

It makes so much sense to play up the nectar-sweet feature of ripe stone fruit, especially with a fruit such as apricot that has plenty of contrasting tanginess. Here, tart apricots are tossed with a honey syrup scented with orange blossom water, also called orange flower water. It's great to have a jar of these waiting in your refrigerator for impromptu desserts. The fragrant treat is absolutely delicious served atop yogurt, ice cream, or a slice of ripe triple-cream cheese.

ORANGE BLOSSOM APRICOTS

MAKES ABOUT 1 CUP [170 G]

3 lb [1.4 kg] fresh apricots, halved and pitted

2 cups [480 ml] water

¼ cup [85 g] honey

2 Tbsp orange blossom water

2 Tbsp fresh lemon juice

1. Line dehydrator trays with non-stick mesh sheets that have been lightly coated with cooking oil.

2. Lay out the apricot halves on the prepared trays. **Dry at 135°F [57°C] for 12 to 24 hours,** until they are chewy, leathery, and not squishy, depending on the size of the fruit. Let cool completely.

3. In a medium nonreactive saucepan over medium-high heat, bring the water and honey to a boil. Turn off the heat and whisk in the orange blossom water and lemon juice. Add the dried apricot halves. Turn the heat back to medium-high and bring to a simmer. Cook, stirring frequently, until the reduced liquid is thick enough to coat a spoon. Let cool completely.

4. Store in an airtight container in the refrigerator for up to 1 month.

In fall, parts of my neighborhood are littered with Italian prune plums, frosty violet on the outside and darkly amber and juicy inside. I seek out friends with backyard trees and gather as much of the fruit as I can for drying, on their own and also first soaked in brandy for a grown-up take on the sugar plum. Don't discard the spiced brandy you use for soaking the plums; it can be reused for future batches, or better yet, sipped as a cordial or as a component in a Champagne cocktail.

DRIED BRANDIED PLUMS

MAKES ABOUT 2 CUPS [380 G]

2 lb [910 g] Italian prune plums, halved and pitted

2 cups [480 ml] brandy

2 Tbsp brown sugar

2 cinnamon sticks

2 star anise

1. In a large bowl, combine the plum halves, brandy, brown sugar, cinnamon, and star anise and stir to mix. Cover and let soak for at least 24 hours, or up to 48 hours. Strain, reserving the spiced brandy for another use. Try pushing the rounded skin side of the plums upward to turn them inside out, which will help them dry faster.

2. Line dehydrator trays with non-stick mesh sheets that have been lightly coated with cooking oil.

3. Lay out the plums cut-side down on the prepared trays. **Dry at 135°F [57°C] for 24 to 28 hours,** until the plums are leathery and no longer squishy at their centers. Some plums will probably dry more quickly than others, so remove those as they are dry, and finish drying the others. Let cool completely. You may choose to condition the plums at this point (see page 21).

4. Store in an airtight container, preferably with a silica gel packet to extend freshness, in a dark place at room temperature for up to 3 months, or in the freezer for up to 1 year.

I am industrious in many ways, but dessert cookery is not one of my strengths. Even though I spent a brief part of my career as a pastry chef, I'm always happy to find a lazy cake or a crumble instead of working up a fancy tart or fussy cookies. Thank heavens for clafouti, a French dessert that lies somewhere between a custard and a cake. Here, I've soaked dried plums in brewed Earl Grey tea for a little nuanced citrus allure to complement the sweet-tart goodness of the fruit. You can also just scoop the tea-plumped prunes over ice cream for an even easier dessert.

EARL GREY PLUM CLAFOUTI

SERVES 6 TO 8

½ cup [190 g] Dried Brandied Plums (page 64)

1 cup [240 ml] hot strong Earl Grey tea

1 Tbsp honey

3 eggs

½ cup [100 g] sugar

¾ cup [180 ml] buttermilk or crème fraîche

¾ cup [180 ml] whole milk

2 tsp vanilla extract

¼ tsp salt

6 Tbsp [45 g] flour

1 Tbsp unsalted butter

1. Position a rack in the upper third of the oven and preheat to to 375°F [190°C]. Butter and flour a 10-in [25-cm] round baking dish or ovenproof skillet.

2. Put the plums in a small saucepan, and pour the tea and honey over them. Let rest for 5 minutes, and then bring to a boil over medium-high heat. Turn the heat to low, and simmer until the liquid is almost all absorbed or evaporated. Let cool completely.

3. In a large bowl, whisk the eggs vigorously with the sugar for about 2 minutes, until the eggs are a paler shade of yellow. Whisk in the buttermilk, milk, vanilla, and salt. Sift the flour into the mixture and stir until just combined.

4. Evenly distribute the plums across the bottom of the prepared pan. Scrape any remaining glaze from the plum pan into the batter and stir to combine. Pour the batter over the plums. Dot the top of the batter with bits of the butter.

5. Bake until the middle of the clafouti is just set, 30 to 35 minutes. Turn on the broiler and cook the clafouti, until the top is puffed and amber-brown in patches, 2 to 3 minutes, watching carefully so it doesn't burn. Transfer to a wire rack to cool.

6. Serve warm or at room temperature.

TIPS FOR COOKING WITH DRIED FRUITS

Dried fruits are the backbone of so many great dishes, both sweet and savory. Here are some ways to use them well.

Savory foods:

If you are looking for new ways to incorporate dried fruit into your cooking, look to recipes like Mexican *moles*, North African *tagines*, and Persian rice dishes and stews (or *khoresh*). In these traditional dishes, the sweet-tart flavor of dried fruit is used to balance the richness of the savory dishes.

Use creatively:

If you have a side dish or a salad that seems drab, sometimes a handful of dried fruit will give you just the right amount of color and verve. Remember that fruit added at the beginning of cooking will be softer, while that added at the end of cooking (or to a salad) will be chewier.

Compotes:

Dried fruit becomes a delicious sauce if you place it in a pan in equal proportion to liquid (water, wine, fruit juice). Sweeten if desired and add in whole spices or citrus zest for extra flavor. Bring to a simmer and cook until the fruit is soft and plump and any juices are nicely thickened.

In baking:

Dried fruit can taste more compelling if it's reconstituted before stirring into cakes, cookies, or breads. This can be as simple as soaking the fruit in hot water for a bit before using it, or you can make the soaking liquid something more fetching, such as tea, coffee, fruit juice, wine, or liqueur.

If you are working dried fruit into a fruit pie, tart, or cobbler, don't soak it first. Let it act as a sponge instead, soaking up the extra liquid from your fruit filling. This is a great trick for warding off runny juices and soggy crusts.

These translucent orange slices are drop-dead beautiful. In fact, I've seen similar slices strung together in garlands forming a pretty decoration for a shop window. A perfect cross section can serve as an exquisite embellishment for cakes, cheese plates, or ice cream, but don't let the decorative appeal keep you from eating it. The chips deliver intense citrus flavor with a surprising, crackly texture. They are also a perfect addition to mulled wine and cider. You can use the thin-slice method for tangerines, grapefruit, and blood oranges, as well, but since we're leaving the skins on, I find that navel oranges offer the best combination of sweetness and bitter tones. These orange slices will be at their crispest in the first two weeks.

ORANGE CHIPS

MAKES 4 CUPS [170 G]

4 navel oranges

2 tsp olive oil

⅛ tsp sea salt

1. Line dehydrator trays with non-stick mesh sheets that have been lightly coated with cooking oil.

2. Slice the oranges crosswise very thinly (⅛ in [3 mm] or less) and place in a medium bowl. It is helpful to use a serrated knife for cutting these thin slices. Gently toss the orange slices with the olive oil and salt.

3. Lay out the orange slices in a single layer on the prepared trays. **Dry at 135°F [57°C] for 12 to 18 hours,** until very dry and crisp. Let cool completely.

4. Store in airtight containers, preferably with a silica gel packet to extend freshness, in a dark place at room temperature for up to 2 months.

All the best drinks have a bitter note, and this is definitely a cocktail-inspired confection—sweet but with considerable depth. Here, the dehydrator serves to speed up the final stage of a traditional candied peel recipe, drying the exterior that wraps around a dense, chewy citrus interior. This basic method works for any citrus peel (zest and pith), and thin slices of ginger too.

CANDIED BITTERED GRAPEFRUIT PEEL

MAKES ABOUT 4 CUPS [120 G]

Peels of 3 grapefruits, cut into ½-in- [12-mm-] wide strips

3 cups [600 g] sugar

¾ tsp Angostura bitters or other bitters

1. Fill a medium nonreactive saucepan with water and bring to a boil. Add the grapefruit peels, cook for 30 seconds, and then drain. Put the peels aside in a bowl. Refill the pot with fresh water and repeat the blanching process twice more.

2. In the same pan over medium-high heat, combine 2 cups [480 ml] water, 2 cups [400 g] of the sugar, and the bitters and stir until the sugar is dissolved. Add the grapefruit peels, turn the heat to medium, and let simmer slowly for 40 to 50 minutes, until the peels are translucent and very tender and shiny. Remove from the heat and let the peels completely cool in the syrup.

3. Drain the grapefruit peels. Fill a small bowl with the remaining 1 cup [200 g] sugar. Toss a few pieces of peel at a time in the sugar, coating them, and then shake off any extra sugar.

4. Line dehydrator trays with nonstick mesh sheets.

5. Lay out the peel pieces on the prepared trays. **Dry at 135°F [57°C] for 1½ hours**, until dry to the touch but still moist in the interior. Let cool completely.

6. Store in airtight containers, preferably with parchment paper between each layer of peels (to prevent sticking) and a silica gel packet to extend freshness, in a dark place at room temperature for up to 1 month.

The sweet warm spices—like fennel, cinnamon, cardamom, and ginger—that infuse tea for chai can be put to other good uses, like for this chewy pineapple treat. Save the sweet marinade in a jar in the refrigerator; it will also work with apples, pears, and mangos, and you can use it to sweeten iced tea or lemonade.

DRIED PINEAPPLE WITH CHAI SPICES

MAKES ABOUT 2 CUPS [50 G]

2 cups [480 ml] water

1 cup [200 g] sugar

¼ tsp fennel seeds

1 cinnamon stick

10 green cardamom pods

Three ½-in- [12-mm-] thick slices peeled fresh ginger

10 cloves

1 pineapple, peeled, cored, and cut into 1-in [2.5-cm] wedges

1. In a medium saucepan over medium-high heat, combine the water, sugar, fennel seeds, cinnamon stick, cardamom pods, ginger, and cloves and bring to a boil. Turn off the heat and add the pineapple. Set aside and let stand until cool. Refrigerate for at least 1 hour, or up to overnight.

2. Line dehydrator trays with non-stick mesh sheets that have been lightly coated with cooking oil.

3. Drain the pineapple, reserving the syrup for another use, if desired. Lay out the pineapple pieces on the prepared trays. **Dry at 135°F [57°C] for 18 to 24 hours,** until the pineapple is dry to the touch and chewy. Let cool completely. You may choose to condition the pineapple at this point (see page 21).

4. Store in an airtight container, preferably with a silica gel packet to extend freshness, in a dark place at room temperature for up to 3 months, or in the freezer for up to 1 year.

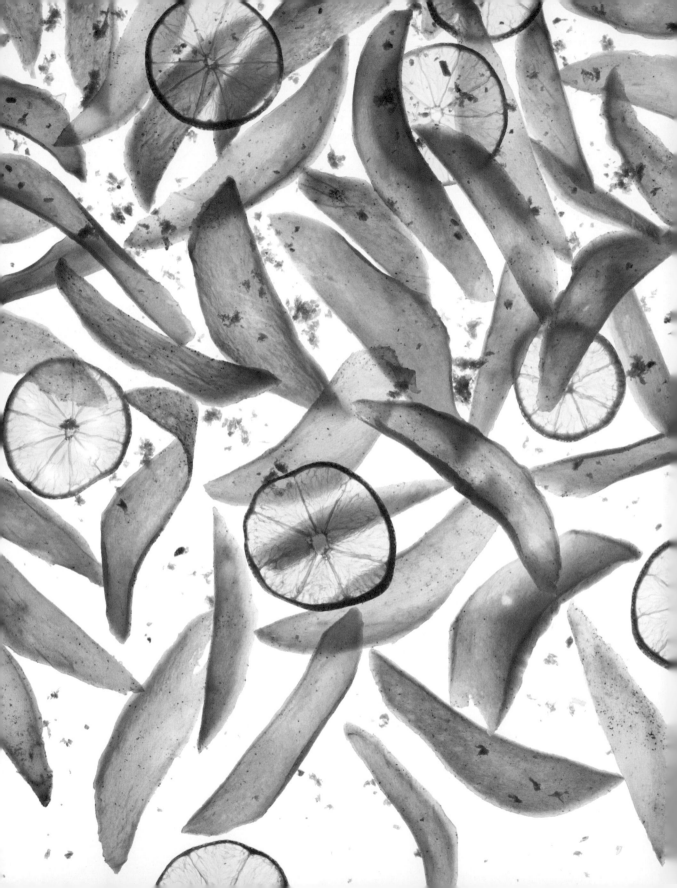

When you get fresh fruit from a vendor at a Mexican market, you'll often have the choice of having it dusted with chile, salt, and a squeeze of lime—little accents that bring out the juicy sweetness of a mango or melon as you slurp it down. I gave that idea another look in this sweet-savory dried fruit combination. Ancho chile powder delivers a mellow aromatic heat, while a touch of optional cayenne pepper will give the mango a more assertive bite. If you really like a puckery experience, dip the dried mango briefly in water and then dip it in the lime powder before eating.

CHILE-LIME MANGOS

MAKES ABOUT 2 CUPS [45 G]

5 tsp fresh lime juice, plus 1 lime, cut in about ⅛-in- [3-mm-] thick slices (optional)

2 tsp agave syrup

¼ tsp ancho chile powder

¼ tsp fine sea salt

Pinch of cayenne pepper (optional)

2 large ripe mangos, peeled, pitted, and cut into ⅜-in [1-cm] slices

1. Line dehydrator trays with non-stick mesh sheets that have been lightly coated with cooking oil.

2. In a large bowl, whisk together the lime juice, agave syrup, ancho chile powder, sea salt, and cayenne (if using). Add the mango slices to the mixture and gently toss to evenly coat.

3. Lay out the mango slices and the lime slices (if using) on the prepared trays. **Dry at 135°F [57°C] for 4 to 6 hours,** until the mango is leathery and dry to the touch and the limes are crisp and snap when bent. Let cool completely.

4. In a spice grinder, working in batches, pulverize the dried lime slices into a very fine powder.

5. Store in airtight containers, preferably with silica gel packets to extend freshness, in a dark place at room temperature for up to 3 months, or in the freezer for up to 1 year.

CHAPTER 3: FRUIT LEATHERS AND PANS

In the Pacific Northwest summers, the supply of delicious local berries is almost limitless. In June, glistening strawberries mound up high on farmers' market tables, followed by precious fragrant raspberries in July. August brings plump blueberries, both wild and cultivated. And September is the time to scout for wild blackberry canes, with their juicy, outsize ripe berries, which grow as weeds in every untended patch of green.

Fruit leather is truly one of the most amusing ways to use your dehydrator. There is something so appealing about the smooth, pliable texture of fruit leathers, and it is a great solution for when you have lots of extra fruit. What follows are several combinations I like. Fruit leathers are a great improvisatory medium. Simply make a cooked or uncooked purée of your favorite fruits, spread it thin on dehydrator trays lined with fruit-leather sheets, and dry until smooth and pliable.

Dried fruit can also be pressed into a Spanish-inspired *pan*, a "bread" of pressed, honeyed fruit and nuts and/or seeds. The flavors and textures of a fruit-nut pan are just right for serving in thin slices with cheese (go with Manchego if you want to keep the Spanish theme). Again, there is an element of play when making a fruit "pan"—you can press it into a rect- angular loaf in a bread pan, make a nice dome by molding it in a bowl, or even make individual "pans" in a muffin tin. And you can always swap one fruit for another—apricots, figs, plums, even peaches would all work well.

There's something about the slight anise flavor of basil that pairs beautifully with plums. Both work together in this fruit leather to make a supremely summery fruit snack. A quick cooking of the plums controls the tannins in them and makes for a lovely rosy purée.

RED PLUM–BASIL LEATHER

MAKES 12 TO 14 PORTIONS

3 lb [1.4 kg] red plums, skins on, pitted, and each cut into 8 pieces

¼ cup [85 g] honey

¼ cup [60 ml] water

10 sprigs fresh basil

1. Put the plums in a large, wide, nonreactive saucepan. Add the honey and water, and stir to combine. Cover and cook over medium heat for about 5 minutes, until the plums are bathed in their own juices. Remove the cover, turn the heat to low, and gently simmer for 5 to 8 minutes, until the plums have softened but are still chunky and brightly colored.

2. Using a blender or a food mill, purée the plums with their liquid. (If using a blender, take care to work in small batches, remove the blender-lid plug to allow air pressure to escape, cover the top with a clean folded towel to prevent spattering and burns, and hold the towel-covered lid down while blending.)

3. Pour the purée into a large bowl to cool, and add the basil sprigs, pushing them below the surface of the plums. Cover and refrigerate for 1 hour.

4. Line dehydrator trays with nonstick fruit-leather sheets.

5. Remove the basil sprigs from the plums and discard. Using an offset spatula or the back of a spoon, spread out the purée on the prepared trays, making the edges a little thicker than the center. **Dry at 135°F [57°C] for 4 to 6 hours**, until dry to the touch on both sides and the leather holds together when peeled off the nonstick sheet. (You can speed up the process by peeling the mixture off the nonstick sheet and turning it over after 3 hours, though this is not necessary.) Run a spatula under the mixture to loosen it, and let cool completely.

6. Peel the fruit leather off the nonstick sheet. Cut into single-serving portions and roll up in plastic wrap or parchment paper. (If using parchment, tie or tape the roll to hold it together.)

7. Store in an airtight container, preferably with a silica gel packet to extend freshness, in a dark place at room temperature for up to 2 weeks, or in the refrigerator for up to 1 month.

POINTERS FOR IMPROVISING WITH FRUIT

Make sure your leather sticks together.

You want to have enough pectin in your fruit purée before drying it so it will dry in a cohesive layer. Some fruits have more pectin than others, which can cause varying final results. Pectin is a polysaccharide found in fruit that has a gelling effect on sweet mixtures; it's the component, for example, that gels fruit preserves. If you are using a low-pectin ingredient like berries or rhubarb, blend in another fruit that has plenty of pectin to ensure the cohesiveness and chewiness you seek. Apples (or applesauce) are high in pectin and never disappoint, and banana gives a mellow, opaque base for good fruit leather.

Sweeten at will.

The ripest fruit often doesn't need any added sugar, but some tart fruit needs a little mellowing. Sugar works, but I prefer honey or agave syrup for sweetening fruit leathers because it fits better with the earthy nature of the final result. Whatever sweetener you use, start with just a touch, then taste, and increase only as needed. Remember, with lots of added sugar, the final product may not dry satisfactorily.

Make fruit leather edges thick.

Spread your fruit purée onto nonstick fruit-leather dehydrator sheets, making the edges thicker than the center. The edges tend to dry out more quickly and will crack if they are too thin.

Add savory elements.

Plain yogurt, tomatoes, turmeric, ginger, and herbs can add interesting flavors to your fruit purées. Use them in small quantities to start, building flavor as you make your fruit-leather recipes.

Have fun.

If you are feeling whimsical, cut pieces of fruit leather with small cookie cutters into shapes to decorate cupcakes or other desserts.

Blackberries and blueberries are abundant and delicious in summer. Sadly, neither berry is a great candidate for drying on its own. They aren't as deliciously chewy after drying as you might expect. When you're confronted with a textural issue such as this with a particular dried fruit, consider making a fruit leather of it. This approach hastens the drying time and smooths out the textural issues. And by combining the two berries in this fruit leather, you get a deliciously chewy treat that's as gorgeously midnight purple as a summer night sky.

BLACKBERRY-BLUEBERRY LEATHER

MAKES 8 TO 10 PORTIONS

1 pt [230 g] blackberries

1 pt [230 g] blueberries

1 cup [240 ml] unsweetened applesauce

2 Tbsp honey

1 Tbsp fresh lemon juice

1. Line dehydrator trays with nonstick fruit-leather sheets.

2. Combine the blackberries, blueberries, applesauce, honey, and lemon juice in a large food processor (or blender). Process into a smooth purée.

3. Using an offset spatula or the back of a spoon, spread out the purée on the prepared trays, making the edges a little thicker than the center. **Dry at 135°F [57°C] for 4 to 6 hours,** until the mixture is leathery and dry to the touch on both sides. (You can speed up the process by peeling the mixture off the nonstick sheet and turning it over after about 3 hours, though this is not necessary.) Run a spatula under the mixture to loosen it, and let cool completely.

4. Peel the fruit leather off the nonstick sheet. Cut into single-serving portions and roll up in plastic wrap or parchment paper. (If using parchment, tie or tape the roll to keep it together.)

5. Store in an airtight container, preferably with a silica gel packet to extend freshness, in a dark place at room temperature for up to 2 weeks, or in the refrigerator for up to 1 month.

My kids sometimes got annoyed with me as I worked my way through new recipes for this book. They do not want chile on their dried mango, or vermouth in their dried cherries—they like their dried foods simple and straightforward. This fruit-leather recipe couldn't be more straightforward. It uses the best of early summer—tangy apricots and raspberries—in one snack. Honey softens the tartness just a bit, and provides just a light note of floral complexity. Add the honey a little at a time, and taste to gauge; apricots vary a great deal in sourness, and you may find you need less honey if you're working with an extra-ripe, sweet variety.

APRICOT-RASPBERRY LEATHER

MAKES 8 TO 10 PORTIONS

1 pt [170 g] raspberries

1½ lb [680 g] apricots, halved and pitted

¼ cup [60 ml] water

2 to 3 Tbsp honey

1. Line dehydrator trays with nonstick fruit-leather sheets.

2. Combine the raspberries, apricots, and water in a large food processor (or blender). Process into a smooth purée. Add 2 Tbsp of the honey and mix well. Taste and decide whether the purée needs more sweetening; if so, add the remaining 1 Tbsp honey.

3. Using an offset spatula or the back of a spoon, spread out the purée on the prepared trays, making the edges a little thicker than the center. **Dry at 135°F [57°C] for 4 to 6 hours**, until the mixture is leathery and dry to the touch both. (You can speed up the process by peeling the mixture off the nonstick sheet and turning it over after about 3 hours, though this is not necessary.) Run a spatula under the mixture to loosen it, and let cool completely.

4. Peel the fruit leather off the nonstick sheet. Cut into single-serving portions and roll up in plastic wrap or parchment paper. (If using parchment, tie or tape the roll to keep it together.)

5. Store in an airtight container, preferably with a silica gel packet to extend freshness, in a dark place at room temperature for up to 2 weeks, or in the refrigerator for up to 1 month.

Rhubarb isn't a fruit—it's a vegetable—but it stands in pretty well for one, and this pretty, pale snack is just the thing in late winter, when rhubarb is the only item in season in your backyard and you're sitting around waiting for spring to arrive. You can get your fruit-leather practice in before the relentless time in the summer when everything gets ripe at once. Here, I used a little banana to provide some leathery structure for the rhubarb, and it mellows out rhubarb's tartness. This is one fruit leather where a little sugar is necessary, since rhubarb on its own is powerfully sour. When preparing rhubarb, cut off and discard any toxic green leaves atop the stalk, and cook only the stalk.

RHUBARB-BANANA LEATHER

MAKES 8 TO 10 PORTIONS

1½ lb [680 g] rhubarb, peeled, cut into ½-in [12-mm] slices

½ cup [120 ml] water

½ cup [100 g] sugar

1 tsp vanilla extract, or 1 vanilla bean

2 ripe bananas, peeled and cut into chunks

1. Line dehydrator trays with nonstick fruit-leather sheets.

2. In a large nonreactive sauce-pan over medium heat, combine the rhubarb, water, and sugar. Add the vanilla and stir. (If using a vanilla bean, slit it in half lengthwise and scrape the seeds into the pan.) Cook, stirring occasionally, until the rhubarb is tender, about 10 minutes.

3. Place the rhubarb mixture in a large blender with the bananas. Blend until the mixture is a very smooth purée that is pale golden pink. Using an offset spatula or the back of a spoon, spread out the purée on the prepared trays, making the edges a little thicker than the center. **Dry at 135°F [57°F] for 6 to 8 hours,** until dry to the touch, rotating the trays at least once. (You can speed up the process by peeling the mixture off the nonstick sheet and turning it over after about 3 hours, though this is not necessary.) Run a spatula under the mixture to loosen it, and let cool completely.

4. Peel the fruit leather off the nonstick sheet. Cut into single-serving portions and roll up in plastic wrap or parchment paper. (If using parchment, tie or tape the roll to keep it together.)

5. Store in an airtight container, preferably with a silica gel packet to extend freshness, in a dark place at room temperature for up to 2 weeks, or in the refrigerator for up to 1 month.

This apricot-almond cake is a tangy take on the fruit *pan* idea. It is a gorgeous golden-orange companion to a voluptuous bloomy cheese like Camembert or Brie. Because the apricots (*albaricoques*) are chopped up, it has a more cohesive texture than the chunky *pan de higo* (page 87). If you can't get fresh apricots, you can make this with already dried apricots.

PAN DE ALBARICOQUE

SERVES 8 TO 10

3 lb [1.4 kg] fresh apricots (or 8 oz [240 g] dried apricots)

½ cup [60 g] almonds

½ tsp ground cinnamon

⅛ tsp ground cardamom

¼ tsp ground cloves

2 Tbsp honey

2 Tbsp brandy or orange liqueur

1. Line dehydrator trays with non-stick mesh sheets that have been lightly coated with cooking oil.

2. Cut the apricots in half, and remove the pits. If the apricots are larger than about 2 in [5 cm] in diameter, cut them into quarters. Lay out the apricots on the prepared trays. **Dry at 135°F [57°C] for 12 to 18 hours**, until the fruit is leathery and does not seem squishy below the skin.

3. Preheat the oven to 300°F [150°C]. Line an 8½-by-4½-in [22-by-11-cm] loaf pan with plastic wrap.

4. Lay out the almonds on a baking sheet and toast for 12 to 14 minutes, until lightly browned through to the center. Let cool completely.

5. Chop the dried apricots coarsely, using a knife or pulsing in a food processor. Scrape the apricots into a medium bowl, and add the cinnamon, cardamom, cloves, honey, and brandy, folding to make a mixture that holds together in clumps when pressed with the spoon. Fold in the almonds.

6. Press the apricot mixture into the prepared loaf pan, making sure to press it firmly into the corners. Rap the pan on the counter to help settle the mixture, and press again. Wrap the ends of the plastic wrap firmly around the *pan*, and press evenly one more time. If you have a second loaf pan with the same dimensions, place it atop the mixture and weigh it down with jars, pie weights, or other weights; the weight will produce a more condensed fruit "bread," but this isn't essential. Leave at room temperature, or in the refrigerator if it's muggy weather in the middle of summer, for 2 days. Remove any weights, then rewrap the *pan* first in parchment and then in clean plastic wrap.

7. Store in the refrigerator for up to 2 months.

Pan de higo, or fig cake, is probably the best-known variation of this Spanish fruit-nut/seed "bread," which is speckled with crunchy fig seeds throughout. It is a wonderful accompaniment to semifirm or firm cheese, especially sheep's-milk varieties like Manchego. Fresh figs are among the longer drying projects, but they're worth it. If you don't feel like drying them yourself, you can give this recipe a whirl with purchased dried figs—I especially like Turkish dried figs.

PAN DE HIGO

SERVES 8 TO 10

2 pt [680 g] fresh ripe figs, stemmed and cut in half (or 8 oz [230 g] dried figs)

½ cup [50 g] walnut halves

¼ tsp anise seeds

¼ tsp fennel seeds

¼ tsp ground cinnamon

Pinch of salt

2 Tbsp brandy

2 Tbsp honey

1. Line dehydrator trays with non-stick mesh sheets that have been lightly coated with cooking oil.

2. Lay out the fig halves on the prepared trays. **Dry at 135°F [57°C] for 12 to 18 hours**, until leathery and no longer squishy. Let cool completely.

3. Preheat the oven to 325°F [165°C]. Line a 2- to 3-cup [480- to 720-ml] bowl with plastic wrap.

4. Lay out the walnut halves on a baking sheet and toast for 12 to 14 minutes, until lightly browned. Let cool completely.

5. Figs need to be pliable to mold well; plump the dried figs a bit by placing them in a microwave-safe bowl with 2 Tbsp water. Cover the bowl with a plate, and microwave on high for 1 minute. Let the figs steam for 5 minutes, and then check their texture again. If they are still tough, microwave one more time. Drain any remaining water.

6. In a medium bowl, toss the figs with the anise seeds, fennel seeds, cinnamon, salt, brandy, and honey.

7. Put a layer of the most attractive fig halves, skin-side down, on the bottom of the prepared bowl. Place a layer of the toasted walnut halves atop that. Press firmly as you go. Place another layer of figs atop the walnuts, pressing firmly. Continue to make layers of figs and nuts, making sure to end with figs. Wrap the ends of the plastic wrap across the top of the figs, and press down firmly to help mold the fig-nut mixture into the shape of the bowl. If you have a similar bowl, place it atop the mixture and weigh it down with jars, pie weights, or other weights; the weight will produce a more condensed fruit "bread," but this isn't essential. Leave at room temperature, or in the refrigerator if it's muggy weather in the middle of summer, for 2 days. Remove any weight then rewrap the *pan* first in parchment and then in clean plastic wrap.

8. Store in the refrigerator for up to 2 months.

CHAPTER 4: VEGETABLES TRANSFORMED

In a fascinating *Saveur* article, Maryam Reshii tells of the Kashmiri winter tradition of cooking with dried greens, turnips, tomatoes, eggplant, and gourds. Even before the widespread use of refrigeration, these long-lasting dried vegetables kept families in good health even as snowy roads kept fresh goods from coming up from the lowlands. Just because these vegetables were survival food doesn't mean they were a chore to eat. The vegetables, full of sun-concentrated flavors, would be reconstituted in toothsome and hearty curries. Reshii writes that even today, the dried winter curries are a powerful comfort food for many Kashmiris. Even if you don't rely on dried vegetables to make it through a rough mountain winter, you, too, can use your dehydrator to store up the nutritious bounty of summer and fall gardens.

If fruit is a natural in the dehydrator, vegetables, with less sugar and acid content, are a little trickier to figure out. With a little dedication, you'll discover quite a few vegetables that are wonderful to eat in dried form. Many of the recipes in this chapter work as healthful, tasty snacks: kale chips coated with garlicky tahini or a dusting of Parmigiano-Reggiano cheese, ribbons of root vegetables graced with a hint of sunny curry powder, or airy zucchini crisps dried with yogurt. Other recipes include dried ingredients that will add depth to kitchen creations, such as caramelized onions that can be sprinkled on a salad for crunch and flavor, or rehydrated in the best onion dip you've tasted. Tomatoes, of course, can be wonderful dried, and here we'll look at two different versions: rustic, skin-on tomatoes marinated in herbed olive oil, and the more elegant, semidried "petals" of plum tomatoes that provide sweet flavor and satisfying texture to pastas, fish dishes, or canapés. This chapter focuses on veggies that taste great in dried or semidried form. And you may want to try drying other vegetables, like peas, thinly sliced asparagus, or beets cut into wedges. Though you might not eat them out of hand, take a cue from those Kashmiri families and stir them into soup, stews, or curries for an extra dose of color and flavor.

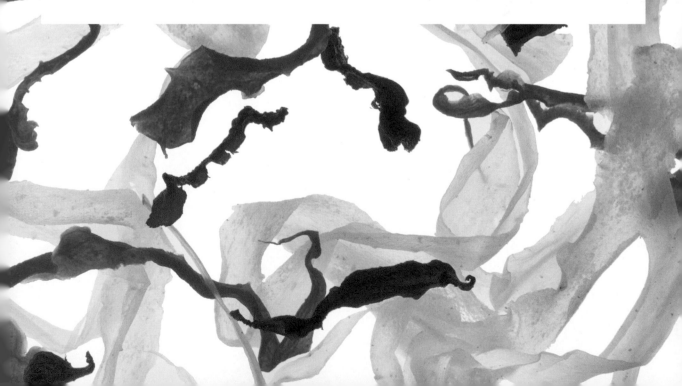

Caramelized onions are the secret to so many flavorful preparations: amazing stews, French onion soup, and delicious sour cream dip. To get that rich flavor, you need to cook onions for a good amount of time, coaxing them to a deep, dark brown, and stirring them before they actually blacken. Take your time and have fun. Once the onions are dried, you can grind them into a rough powder that you can pack into the woods with a morsel of dried bouillon for a cup for delicious soup on the go. Or soak them in a bit of water and fold them into ground meat for an especially savory meatloaf.

DRIED CARAMELIZED ONIONS

MAKES ABOUT 1¼ CUPS [175 G]

1 Tbsp butter

1 Tbsp olive or canola oil

2 lb [910 g] onions, peeled, trimmed, and sliced thinly

4 fresh thyme sprigs

1 tsp fine sea salt

¼ tsp freshly ground black pepper

1 cup [240 ml] off-dry sherry, or white wine like Riesling

1. In a large, heavy-bottomed frying pan over medium heat, warm the butter and olive oil. Add the onions and thyme sprigs and toss well. Cook undisturbed until the onions begin to brown. Stir with a wooden spoon, scraping up any sticky brown bits from the bottom of the pan. Turn the heat to medium-low, add the salt and pepper, and continue to cook, stirring and scraping when a brown layer accumulates in the pan. If the brown layer is blackening quickly, turn the heat to low. After about 30 minutes of cooking, add in ½ cup [120 ml] of the sherry, and thoroughly scrape the bottom of the pan. After another 10 minutes, add the remaining ½ cup [120 ml] sherry and scrape again. Continue cooking until the onions are very soft and an even chestnut brown. (If at any point the onions darken too much, stir in a splash of water and scrape the pot again.) Let cool and discard the thyme sprigs.

2. Line dehydrator trays with nonstick fruit-leather sheets.

3. Lay out the onion mixture on the prepared trays, and press down to make as thin a layer as possible. **Dry at 135°F [57°C] for 14 to 18 hours,** until the onions are crackly brittle. Some thicker areas may be more pliable, but the edges should crack off. Let cool completely.

4. Peel the dried onion layer off the nonstick sheet and break into smaller pieces. If desired, in a spice grinder or food processor, working in batches, grind into a coarse powder. It is okay to leave some larger morsels of onion; they will be very soft when rehydrated.

5. Store in an airtight container, preferably with a silica gel packet to extend freshness, in a dark place at room temperature for up to 3 months, or in the freezer for up to 1 year.

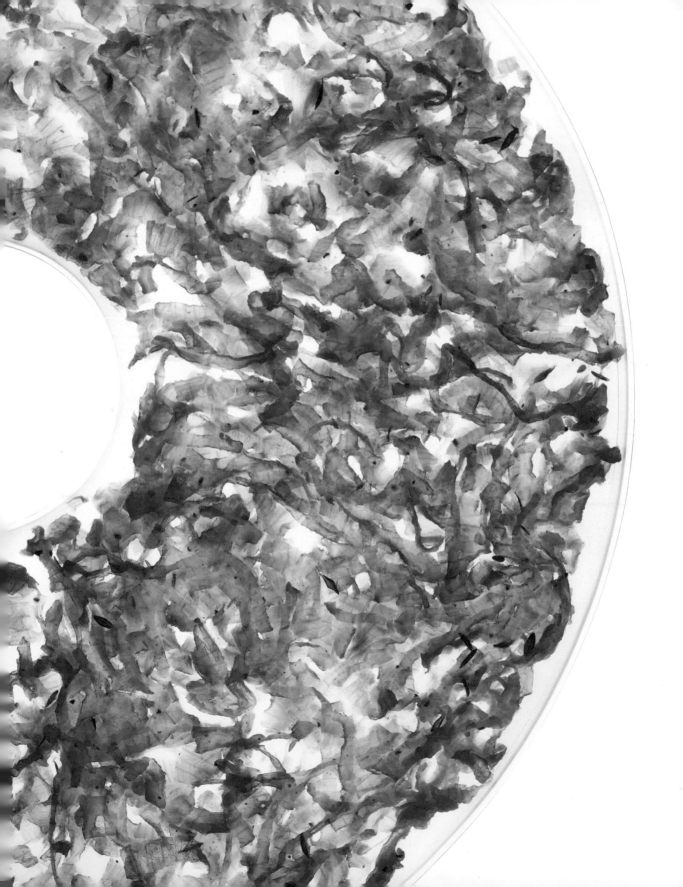

This dip is so crazy good with potato chips. I like a thick dip but, if you prefer a slightly thinner texture, feel free to thin it with cream or buttermilk. If you want to spread it on a freshly baked potato, keep it nice and dense so it will melt extravagantly into the fluffy spud.

CARAMELIZED ONION DIP

MAKES ABOUT 1 CUP [240 G]

¼ cup [35 g] Dried Caramelized Onions (page 90), ground into powder

1 cup [240 ml] crème fraîche

½ tsp sea salt

In a small bowl, mix together the dried onions, crème fraîche, and salt. Let stand at least 30 minutes before serving.

I'm not going to lie, I was trying to make wasabi peas. But with home dehydrators, unlike industrial freeze dryers, you're not always guaranteed a crunch. Sometimes you get a leathery texture, like jerky or dried apricots, and sometimes you get dense morsels of food that are only good for rehydrating. That's what happened with my wasabi peas. But I still loved the idea of a green crunchy snack with big umami flavor, so I worked out this recipe using slivered green beans tossed with a ginger-garlic-soy marinade. I think you'll find they go with a crisp lager almost as well as wasabi peas. Please note that as with many dehydrator-crisped treats, these beans are best eaten soon after they are dried; they soon start to lose their crunch.

GINGER-SOY GREEN BEAN CRISPS

MAKES 4 TO 6 SNACK SERVINGS

1 lb [455 g] fresh green beans, stemmed, strings removed if needed, and cut diagonally into ¼-in- [6-mm-] wide slivers

2 Tbsp soy sauce

1 garlic clove, peeled and minced

1 tsp grated peeled fresh ginger

½ tsp sesame oil

1. Line dehydrator trays with non-stick mesh sheets that have been lightly coated with cooking oil.

2. Bring a pot of salted water to a boil over medium-high heat. Add the green beans and cook until crisp-tender, about 2 minutes. Strain, and then run cool water over the beans for about 1 minute to stop the cooking process.

3. In a medium nonreactive bowl, whisk together the soy sauce, garlic, ginger, and sesame oil. Add the drained beans and toss. Let marinate, stirring once or twice, for 15 minutes. Drain the green beans, reserving the dressing to serve as a rice or noodle condiment.

4. Lay out the green beans on the prepared trays. **Dry at 135°F [57°C] for 4 to 6 hours**, until the beans are very dry and crisp. Let cool completely.

5. Store in an airtight container, preferably with a silica gel packet to extend freshness, in a dark place at room temperature for up to 2 weeks.

I often like to triple up on sesame flavor, as with these kale crisps, which use curly kale for crackly, ruffled edges. In the marinade, I combine tahini, the sesame paste you may have around from making a batch of hummus, with the stir-fry staple, sesame oil. Then, I toss in a handful of toasted sesame seeds for extra texture.

SESAME KALE CRISPS

MAKES 4 TO 6 SNACK SERVINGS

1 Tbsp tahini

¼ tsp sesame oil

1 Tbsp olive oil

½ tsp fine sea salt

1 Tbsp fresh lemon juice

1 garlic clove, peeled and minced

1 head curly kale, washed, stemmed, and torn into 2- to 3-in [5- to 7.5-cm] pieces

1 Tbsp toasted sesame seeds

1. Line dehydrator trays with non-stick mesh sheets that have been lightly coated with cooking oil.

2. In a small bowl, whisk together the tahini, sesame oil, olive oil, salt, lemon juice, and garlic.

3. Put the kale in a large bowl. Pour the tahini dressing over the leaves and massage it thoroughly into the kale leaves. Toss with the sesame seeds.

4. Lay out the kale pieces on the prepared trays. **Dry at 135°F [57°C] for 5 to 7 hours**, until all parts of the kale are dry. Let cool completely.

5. Store in an airtight container, preferably with a silica gel packet to extend freshness, in a dark place at room temperature for up to 3 days.

Kale crisps are really good, but they need a little something to loosen them up. I find that, as with so many things, Parmesan cheese helps. Suddenly the dark green minerality of the crispy kale is in perfect balance with the finger-licking umami goodness of the cheese. Use a rasp-style grater (like a Microplane) to get delicate bits of cheese that will adhere easily.

PARMESAN KALE CRISPS

MAKES 4 TO 6 SNACK SERVINGS

1 head Lacinato (dinosaur or Tuscan) kale washed, stemmed, and cut across into 2-in [5-cm] slices

¼ cup [20 g] freshly grated Parmigiano-Reggiano cheese

¼ tsp red pepper flakes

1 Tbsp fresh lemon juice

1 Tbsp olive oil

½ tsp fine sea salt

1. Line dehydrator trays with non-stick mesh sheets that have been lightly coated with cooking oil.

2. In a large bowl, toss the kale with the Parmigiano-Reggiano, red pepper flakes, lemon juice, olive oil, and salt. Massage the mixture into the kale, making sure all surfaces are well coated.

3. Lay out the kale pieces on the prepared trays. **Dry at 135°F [57°C] for 5 to 7 hours,** until all parts of the kale are dry. Let cool completely.

4. Store in an airtight container, preferably with a silica gel packet to extend freshness, in a dark place at room temperature for up to 3 days.

I'm often hunting for healthier snacks to satisfy my mid-afternoon munchies. Here, thin slices of winter squash dry into savory wafer-thin half-moons. Slicing slippery squash is made much easier with a sturdy mandoline or even a sturdy vegetable peeler. If you work with a knife, try dividing the squash into smaller pieces before slicing very thinly. Thicker pieces are still delicious, but when dried, tend to be more leathery than crisp, so those are better for reconstituting in a cup of miso soup than for pure snacking. If you have Umami Dust on hand, I highly recommend tossing some of it in with the butternut slices. It will give the crisps a mysterious and delightful savory quality.

SPICY BUTTERNUT CRISPS

MAKES 6 TO 8 SNACK SERVINGS

1 medium butternut squash, peeled, seeded, and cut into ⅛-in [3-mm] or thinner slices

1 Tbsp olive oil

1¼ tsp fine sea salt

1½ tsp hot sauce, like Crystal, or to taste

4 tsp Umami Dust (page 30; optional)

2 Tbsp pepitas (shelled pumpkin seeds)

1. Line dehydrator trays with non-stick mesh sheets that have been lightly coated with cooking oil.

2. In a medium bowl, toss the butternut squash slices with the olive oil, salt, hot sauce, and umami dust (if using). Make sure all slices are evenly coated.

3. Lay out the squash slices on the prepared trays. **Dry at 135°F [57°C] for 18 to 24 hours.** To judge doneness, remove a slice and let cool for a few minutes; if it snaps easily, the chips are ready. Let cool completely.

4. In a dry skillet over medium heat, toast the pepitas for 1 to 2 minutes, until they start to crackle and are aromatic. Let cool completely.

5. In a medium bowl, toss the toasted pepitas with the dried butternut slices.

6. Store in an airtight container, preferably with a silica gel packet to extend freshness, in a dark place at room temperature for up to 4 days.

I'm always more charmed by the thought of ranch dressing than the quality of the actual dressing I find at the salad bar. These crispy snacks try to rectify that gap. Tangy, fresh, and sparkling with herb flavor, they are closer to my ranch ideal. It doesn't hurt that they are pretty to look at, too. You could serve them as "croutons" on a salad or as an unconventional garnish on a salmon plate. A bowlful of these crisps works well as a bar snack, too. This is one of those recipes where a sturdy mandoline will make preparation much quicker.

TANGY ZUCCHINI CRISPS

MAKES 4 TO 6 SNACK SERVINGS

¼ cup [60 ml] plain yogurt

½ tsp sea salt

1 garlic clove, peeled and grated

1 Tbsp minced fresh dill

1 lb [455 g] fresh zucchini, very thinly sliced crosswise

1. Line dehydrator trays with non-stick fruit-leather sheets. Also have ready mesh sheets that have been lightly coated with cooking oil.

2. In a medium bowl, whisk together the yogurt, salt, garlic, and dill. Add the sliced zucchini and toss with the yogurt mixture, making sure to evenly coat all the slices.

3. Lay out the zucchini slices on the prepared trays. **Dry at 135°F [57°C] for 2 to 4 hours**, until almost completely dry and crisp. Remove the crisps from the dehydrator, leaving the machine turned on. Peel the slices from the fruit-leather sheets and lay out on the mesh sheets. Return to the dehydrator for 30 minutes to 1 hour, until completely crisp. Let cool completely.

4. Store in an airtight container, preferably with a silica gel packet to extend freshness, in a dark place at room temperature for up to 3 days.

These crunchy nibbles are given a brick-red dusting of pimentón (Spanish smoked paprika), and they make for a most satisfying little bar snack or can be a crunchy garnish for salads. For maximum crispiness, make sure to dry them until they are crackly dry. Dried chickpeas will look darker and most will have a noticeable split in the middle.

PIMENTÓN CHICKPEAS

MAKES 4 TO 6 SNACK SERVINGS

One 15-oz [425-g] can chickpeas (garbanzo beans), rinsed and drained

1 Tbsp olive oil

1 garlic clove, peeled and minced

½ tsp fine sea salt

⅛ tsp freshly ground black pepper

1 tsp pimentón

1. Line dehydrator trays with non-stick mesh sheets that have been lightly coated with cooking oil.

2. In a large bowl, toss the chickpeas with the olive oil, garlic, salt, pepper, and pimentón. Mix thoroughly to coat all the chickpeas. Let marinate for at least 1 hour, or up to overnight. (Refrigerate if more than 2 hours).

3. Lay out the chickpeas on the prepared trays. **Dry at 135°F [57°C] for 18 to 20 hours**, until completely dry and crispy. Let cool completely.

4. Store in an airtight container, preferably with a silica gel packet to extend freshness, in a dark place at room temperature for up to 1 week.

There are few vegetables prettier in cross section than a finely sliced fennel bulb. This recipe presents the layered bulb to full advantage, sliced paper-thin and dried to a chewy crispness. Poised between savory and sugary, these crisped fennel fans work best as a delicious frivolity—as a garnish on a sorbet or a cheese plate, topped with a little smoked salmon and chèvre as an appetizer, or as a little sweet nothing on the side of a cup of tea.

DRIED SWEET FENNEL FANS

MAKES ABOUT 1¾ CUPS [65 G]

2 cups [480 ml] water

2 Tbsp fresh lemon juice, plus 1 Meyer lemon, thinly sliced crosswise

⅔ cup [130 g] sugar

1 tsp fennel seeds

2 large fennel bulbs, trimmed, sliced thinly, cores intact

1. Line dehydrator trays with non-stick mesh sheets that have been lightly coated with cooking oil.

2. In a large nonreactive sauce-pan over medium-high heat, bring the water to a boil. Add the lemon juice, lemon slices, sugar, and fennel seeds. Turn the heat to medium-low and simmer, stirring occasionally, until the sugar dissolves. Add the fennel slices and gently stir to ensure all slices are coated with the lemon-sugar syrup. Simmer gently on low heat for 10 minutes. Drain, reserving the liquid, if desired, for another use.

3. Lay out the fennel fans and the lemon slices on the prepared trays. **Dry at 135°F [57°C] for 14 to 16 hours,** until a cooled piece of fennel is crisp-chewy. Let cool completely.

4. Store in an airtight container, preferably with a silica gel packet to extend freshness, in a dark place at room temperature for up to 2 weeks.

This recipe may win the prize for prettiest bar snack: A pile of airy ruffles in dark burgundy, saffron orange, and ivory white. I have found a sturdy, sharp peeler is a great tool for prepping dehydrating projects, and here I put mine to good use reducing solid root vegetables to whisper-thin strips. Blanching the vegetables before drying helps to unify their textures, and it also hurries along the drying. Like many of the crisp vegetable snacks in this chapter, it is best to eat these soon after drying when they are at their most crisp. However, slightly less-crisp ribbons can be stirred into soups for extra flavor and nutrition.

CURRIED PARSNIP, CARROT, AND BEET RIBBONS

MAKES 4 TO 6 SNACK SERVINGS

2 medium parsnips, peeled

2 medium carrots, peeled

1 small beet, peeled

1 Tbsp olive oil

½ tsp curry powder

¾ tsp sea salt

1. Line dehydrator trays with non-stick mesh sheets that have been lightly coated with cooking oil.

2. Bring a large pot of salted water to a boil over medium-high heat. Fill a large bowl with ice water.

3. While the water is heating, use a sharp peeler to make ribbons of the parsnips, leaving behind the woody center. Repeat to make carrot ribbons, and set aside separately. Repeat to make beet ribbons.

4. Place the parsnip ribbons in the boiling water and cook for 30 seconds. Using a slotted spoon or a spider, remove the ribbons and put them directly into the ice water. After the parsnip ribbons have cooled, lift them from the water and lay them flat on a clean kitchen towel to dry. Repeat with the carrot ribbons, and then with the beet ribbons, keeping each vegetable separate.

5. In a small skillet over medium heat, add the olive oil and curry powder and stir to combine. When the oil becomes fragrant, after about 1½ minutes, remove from the heat.

6. In a medium bowl, stir the parsnip ribbons with about one-third of the curry oil and about ¼ tsp of the salt and toss well. Repeat with the carrot ribbons, and then with the beet ribbons.

Continued

7. Lay out the vegetable ribbons on the prepared trays. **Dry at 135°F [57°C]**, until ruffled and completely crisp. Parsnips should be done in 6 to 8 hours, and carrots and beets may take 8 to 10 hours. Let cool completely.

8. Peel the vegetable ribbons from the nonstick sheets, and mix together on the work surface.

9. Store in an airtight container, preferably with a silica gel packet to extend freshness, in a dark place at room temperature for up to 1 week.

Removing water from juicy fruits and vegetables concentrates their flavors deliciously. These dried, puckered, chewy-moist tomatoes taste robust and tangy on crostini, pizza, pasta, and sandwiches. Packed in a pretty jar, they make a wonderful gift to present to your host at a dinner party.

DRIED MARINATED CHERRY TOMATOES

MAKES ABOUT 1½ CUPS [375 G]

3 cups [455 g] fresh cherry or grape tomatoes

½ tsp sea salt

1 Tbsp balsamic vinegar

2 sprigs thyme

1 sprig rosemary

2 small dried chiles, such as chiles de arbol or japones

1 cup [240 ml] olive oil, plus more if needed

1. Line dehydrator trays with non-stick mesh sheets that have been lightly coated with olive oil.

2. Bring a medium pot of water to a soft boil over medium-high heat. Place the tomatoes in the water and cook until most of their skins split, 1 to 2 minutes. Drain, rinse in cool water, and drain again. If any tomatoes have not split, use a small knife to score the skin. Be careful; hot tomatoes can squirt.

3. Lay out the tomatoes on the prepared trays. **Dry at 135°F [57°C] for 22 to 24 hours**, until the tomatoes are wrinkled and no longer squishy when pinched, but not dried to toughness. Put in a medium bowl.

4. Toss the warm tomatoes with the sea salt and vinegar. Layer the thyme sprigs, rosemary sprig, and chiles in a 1-pt [480-ml] jar. Add the tomatoes, and pour in the olive oil, making sure the tomatoes are covered completely by the oil; add a bit more oil if necessary. Let the dried tomatoes marinate in the olive oil at room temperature for about 24 hours, then transfer to the refrigerator.

5. Store in the refrigerator for up to 1 month.

This recipe makes the most elegant dried tomatoes I have ever seen. The skin is peeled off plum tomatoes and their pulp is scooped out, leaving only the meaty tomato flesh "fillets." Drying the tomato fillets for a few hours in a relatively hot dehydrator intensely concentrates the tomato flavor without making them too chewy or leathery. Once you have these perfect red tomato petals, what do you do with them? Roll them up with dabs of goat cheese for an appetizer; chop them and toss with angel hair pasta, olive oil, and basil for an intense version of a fresh pasta sauce; or garnish a fancy fish dish with them. They are special, and definitely worth the fuss.

SEMIDRIED TOMATO PETALS

MAKES ABOUT 4 OZ [115 G]

16 plum tomatoes

1 tsp fine sea salt

2 Tbsp olive oil, plus more if needed

1½ tsp fresh thyme leaves

1. Line dehydrator trays with nonstick fruit-leather sheets.

2. Bring a large pot of water to a soft boil over medium-high heat. Fill a large bowl with ice water.

3. Score an X through the skin at the pointed end of each tomato. When the water boils, place about four tomatoes in the pot. After about 45 seconds, use a slotted spoon or spider to remove the tomatoes and put them directly into the ice water. Peel the blanched tomatoes. Let the water boil again, and repeat the process with the remaining tomatoes.

4. When peeled, cut each tomato into quarters. Scoop out and discard the seeds and pulp of each quarter. Put the fleshy tomato petals in a large bowl and season with the salt. Toss gently with the olive oil and thyme.

5. Lay out the tomato petals on the prepared trays. **Dry at 160°F [71°C] for 2 to 4 hours,** until the tomatoes have a somewhat matte surface and have shrunk by about half. Let cool completely.

6. Store in an airtight container in the refrigerator for up to 3 days, or cover completely with olive oil and store in the refrigerator for up to 1 month.

Roasted red bell peppers dry beautifully into a sort of vegetarian jerky. Tasty on its own, it's also a great building block for other savory dishes. You can roast the peppers any way you like. Sometimes I char mine over a hot charcoal fire, sometimes over my stove-top gas burners, and sometimes in the oven, which is the least-fiery method and the one used here.

DRIED ROASTED RED BELL PEPPERS

MAKES ABOUT 3 OZ [85 G]

4 red bell peppers

1. Line dehydrator trays with non-stick mesh sheets that have been lightly coated with cooking oil.

2. Adjust the oven racks to sit 8 to 12 in [20 to 30.5 cm] from the upper heating element and preheat the broiler.

3. Place the whole bell peppers on a baking sheet and broil. When one side is blistered and blackened, rotate the pepper to expose another side. Continue broiling and turning the peppers for 15 to 20 minutes, until blistered and blackened on all sides. Remove to a heatproof bowl, cover the bowl with a large plate, and let the peppers steam and cool for 30 minutes. Peel the charred skin from the peppers, pull or cut each pepper into quarters, and remove and discard their stems, pith, and seeds.

4. Lay out the pepper quarters flat on the prepared trays. **Dry at 135°F [57°C] for 10 to 14 hours,** until leathery and a bit crisp.

5. Store in an airtight container, preferably with a silica gel packet to extend freshness, in a dark place at room temperature for up to 3 months, or in the freezer for up to 6 months.

Harissa may be my favorite condiment. This spicy pepper paste comes to us by way of Tunisia, although variations on the hot sauce are popular throughout North Africa and beyond. Somewhere along the line, I discovered a version that included dried rose petals, which added a fragrant, slightly bitter earthiness to the piquant sauce. (I'm not the only one struck by this combination. My friend Renee Erickson, a Seattle chef, included her own version of a rose-infused harissa in her 2014 book *A Boat, A Whale, and A Walrus*.) I slathered it on eggs, lamb, flatbreads, and grilled zucchini, and I vowed to make my own the next time my rosebush bloomed. I think you'll like it too. If you don't have your own rosebush, or access to unsprayed roses from a friend or organic flower grower, look for dried rose petals at Middle Eastern spice stores or websites. Cut the volume in half if you use commercial rose petals, since they tend to be compacted.

ROSE HARISSA

MAKES ABOUT 1 CUP [150 G]

DRIED ROSE PETALS

6 cups [135 g] unsprayed fresh rose petals or ½ cup [3 g] commercial food-grade dried rose petals

2 Dried Roasted Red Bell Peppers (facing page)

5 small dried hot chile peppers, such as chiles de árbol or japones

1 dried pasilla or ancho chile pepper

1½ tsp coriander seeds

1½ tsp caraway seeds

1½ tsp cumin seeds

1 garlic clove, peeled and minced

Fine sea salt

½ cup [120 ml] olive oil, plus more to cover if necessary

1. Line dehydrator trays with nonstick mesh sheets.

2. Pick over the rose petals and discard any leaves, unsightly petals, or bugs.

3. Lay out the petals in single layers on the prepared trays. Dry at 125°F [52°C] for 36 to 48 hours, until completely dry and crisp. Let cool completely.

4. In a small bowl, cover the dried bell peppers, hot chile peppers, and pasilla chile with boiling water. Let soak for 20 minutes, until tender, and then drain. Remove and discard any stems and seeds from the chiles, and chop roughly.

5. In a dry skillet over medium heat, toast the coriander seeds, caraway seeds, and cumin seeds for 30 seconds to 1 minute, until lightly browned and occasionally crackling. Remove from the heat

and lay the dried rose petals across the warm spices while they cool.

6. In a spice grinder, working in batches, pulverize the spices and the rose petals into powder. Set aside.

7. In a food processor (or blender), add the garlic, salt, chile mixture, and spice mixture and pulse to blend, about 30 seconds. With the processor on low, pour in the olive oil, stopping occasionally to scrape down the bowl, until the mixture becomes a coarse paste. Taste and season with more salt, if desired.

8. Spoon the sauce into an airtight glass jar. The pepper mixture should be covered with olive oil to prevent oxidization. If there is not quite enough oil in the mixture, pour a bit more on top of the sauce.

9. Store in the refrigerator for up to 2 weeks.

CHAPTER 5: JERKY

If you were lucky enough to have fresh meat or fish in the pre-industrial age, there was only so much you could eat before it started to go bad. And so, no doubt through accident at first, people realized they could extend the life of their meat by drying it. Now we have refrigeration to help us out, so making jerky at home is all about skipping the preservatives and heavy processing of store-bought jerky, and making incredibly tasty meaty snacks.

Drying meat and fish is a simple process. Removing the water from the cells of the meat hinders the growth of bacteria, and makes for a longer-lasting source of nutrition. Salt also inhibits the growth of harmful bacteria in meat. Drying was also often used in tandem with a more complex process of fermentation, which we won't get into here, but that's how dry salami comes into being. Whether you're looking for a Paleo-friendly snack, preserving the bounty of a beef hindquarter, or just wanting the chewy, carnivorous delights of jerky, you'll have a great time processing it with the dehydrator.

Some dehydration experts recommend cooking meat before drying it, but (with a couple of exceptions) I think that process detracts from the deliciousness of the dried product. At any rate, you will want to follow some sensible rules (see page 112) to make your dried meat experience a safe one.

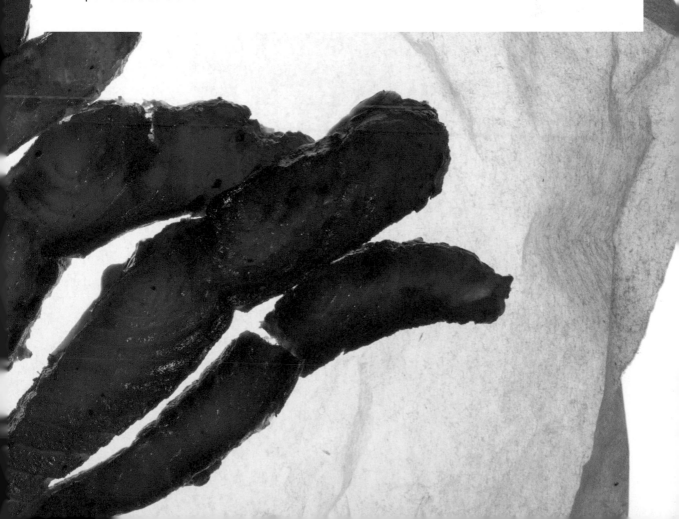

RULES FOR DEHYDRATING MEAT

Keep it clean.

Keep scrupulously clean tools, work surface, and hands when you work with raw meat. Make sure to scrub the dehydrator trays with hot soapy water after use. For extra cleanliness, soak them in a mild bleach solution or, if they are dishwasher safe, run them through the machine.

Keep it hot.

Generally, you want to use the hottest setting on your dehydrator for drying meat so that food spends minimal time in the "danger zone" of 40° to 140°F [4° to 60°C], the environment in which bacteria can cause food-borne illness.

Use good, fresh meat.

Get good meat from a farmer or butcher you trust. You don't want to use discounted meat with an almost expired sell-by date when dehydrating meat.

Grind it yourself.

Ground meat has much more surface area that, when exposed to the environment, can be more problematic in terms of food safety than whole cuts. If you're going to make jerky from ground meat, it's wise to use a food processor or your meat grinder to grind your meat right before you dry it rather than use ground meat from the grocer.

Trim the fat.

Fat takes much longer to dry than muscle, and it will spoil sooner, too, so save the heavily marbled meat for other preparations. For jerky, choose lean cuts like top round and lamb leg, or game meats like elk or bison that are naturally lean.

Consider the jerky gun.

If you like a more tender consistency to your jerky, you may want to consider getting a jerky gun, which extrudes meat in nice, even ribbons (or Slim Jim–size tubes). If you use a jerky gun, you may want to extrude the meat onto nonstick fruit-drying sheets or strips, so it doesn't fall apart on the mesh of the drying tray.

Dry to the right consistency.

My husband prefers jerky that is hard and crispy, but I like it softer and a little more, well, jerk-y. To achieve that flexible consistency, you want your jerky totally dried to the touch but still a bit pliable.

Store it right.

It is fine to take homemade jerky on a backpacking trip, but for longer-term storage, keep it in the freezer or refrigerator. That's the safest bet and, more important, it's the tastiest way to retain that fresh flavor.

All over Seattle, fine-dining enthusiasts and tipsy club-hoppers alike have a hard time resisting the sweet soy call of teriyaki, sold in corner shops all around the city. It just may be my hometown's most popular cheap meal (though Vietnamese sandwiches, *banh mi,* give it solid competition). The combination of soy sauce and ginger is a natural fit as a jerky marinade. In this recipe, I tone down the sugar a bit so that the jerky dries well and isn't too cloying.

TERIYAKI BEEF JERKY

MAKES ABOUT 1 LB [455 G]

2 lb [910 g] beef top round (London broil), fat trimmed

One 4-in [10-cm] piece of ginger, sliced into ½-in [12-mm] discs

3 garlic cloves, peeled and roughly chopped

1 bunch green onions, green tops only

1 small dried chile pepper, such as japones

1 cup [240 ml] mirin (Japanese rice wine) or sherry

¾ cup [180 ml] soy sauce

4 tsp kosher salt

¼ tsp freshly ground black pepper

2 Tbsp brown sugar

1. Put the beef in the freezer for about 1 hour, until it is firm but not rigid. This will facilitate slicing the meat thinly. Cut the meat diagonally across the grain into ⅛-in [3-mm] slices.

2. In a small saucepan over medium-high heat, combine the ginger, garlic, green onions, chile, mirin, soy sauce, salt, pepper, and brown sugar and bring to a boil. Turn the heat to low, stir, and simmer for 2 minutes. Remove from the heat and let cool completely. Strain the marinade, pour over the sliced beef, and toss to coat. Cover and refrigerate overnight.

3. Line dehydrator trays with non-stick mesh sheets that have been lightly coated with cooking oil.

4. Lay out the beef slices flat on the prepared trays. **Dry at 160° to 165°F [71° to 74°C] for 3 to 5 hours**, until evenly darkened, completely matte, and stiffened but still a bit pliable. (A cooled slice of jerky should crack when bent but should not break.) Flip the strips once and rotate the trays once or twice during drying. Remove from the dehydrator and wrap the jerky slices in paper towels to absorb any excess fat. Let cool completely.

5. Store in an airtight container, preferably with a silica gel packet to extend freshness, in a dark place at room temperature for up to 1 week, in the refrigerator for up to 2 weeks, or in the freezer for up to 6 months.

I love to be the one to carve a Sunday beef roast, largely because it gives me nibbling access to the flavorful crusty outer edges. I think of this recipe for basic beef jerky as a way to re-create that chewy, slightly spicy, delicious part of the roast. Good old-fashioned garlic powder, salt, pepper, and bit of smoky paprika make for a wonderful seasoning combination that lends a bit of Sunday roast appeal even when you're trekking along a rugged trail or satisfying an afternoon snack craving.

SALT-AND-PEPPER BEEF JERKY

MAKES ABOUT 1¼ LB [570 G]

2½ lb [1.2 kg] beef top round, fat trimmed

3¾ tsp kosher salt

½ tsp freshly ground black pepper

1 tsp Basic Garlic Powder (page 24)

½ tsp smoked paprika or 1 tsp paprika

1. Put the beef in the freezer for about 1 hour, until it is firm but not rigid. This will facilitate slicing the meat thinly. Cut the meat diagonally across the grain into ⅛-in [3-mm] slices.

2. In a large bowl, stir together the salt, pepper, garlic powder, and paprika. Toss the beef slices with the salt mixture, making sure to separate the slices so the seasoning gets evenly distributed. Cover and refrigerate overnight.

3. Line dehydrator trays with non-stick mesh sheets that have been lightly coated with cooking oil.

4. Lay out the beef slices flat on the prepared trays. **Dry at 160° to 165°F [71° to 74°C] for 3 to 5 hours**, until evenly darkened, completely matte, and stiffened but still a bit pliable. (A cooled slice of jerky should crack when bent but should not break.) Flip the strips once and rotate the trays once or twice during drying. Remove from the dehydrator and wrap the jerky slices in paper towels to absorb any excess fat. Let cool completely.

5. Store in an airtight container, preferably with a silica gel packet to extend freshness, in a dark place at room temperature for up to 1 week, in the refrigerator for up to 2 weeks, or in the freezer for up to 6 months.

Bite into this jerky, and it's easy to imagine that you're resting at a campsite amid scrubby chaparral and the campfire is sending up wisps of musky smoke. Because jerky doesn't typically get smoked as it is created, I often like to sneak a bit of smokehouse flavor into my marinades by adding smoky condiments. Chipotle chile peppers are actually smoked jalapeños, and they are cheap, easy to find, and pack a world of flavor into a small can. There is so much flavor, in fact, that you won't even use a whole can of peppers for a batch of jerky. Try puréeing any leftover chipotle in the blender with mayonnaise to make a spicy sandwich spread.

CHIPOTLE-GARLIC BEEF JERKY

MAKES ABOUT 1¼ LB [570 G]

2½ lb [1.2 kg] beef top round, fat trimmed

¼ cup [60 g] minced chipotle chile pepper in adobo sauce

1 Tbsp olive oil

1 garlic clove, peeled and minced

3¾ tsp kosher salt

1. Put the beef in the freezer for about 1 hour until it is firm but not rigid. This will facilitate slicing the meat thinly. Cut the meat diagonally across the grain into ⅛-in [3-mm] slices.

2. In a large bowl, stir together the chipotle chile, olive oil, garlic, and salt. Toss the beef slices in the chipotle mixture, making sure to separate the slices so the seasoning gets evenly distributed. Cover and refrigerate overnight, or up to 24 hours.

3. Line dehydrator trays with non-stick mesh sheets that have been lightly coated with cooking oil.

4. Lay out the beef slices flat on the prepared trays. **Dry at 160° to 165°F [71° to 74°C] for 3 to 5 hours**, until evenly darkened, completely matte, and stiffened but still a bit pliable. (A cooled slice of jerky should crack when bent but should not break.) Flip the strips once and rotate the trays once or twice during drying. Remove from the dehydrator and wrap the jerky slices in paper towels to absorb any excess fat. Let cool completely.

5. Store in an airtight container, preferably with a silica gel packet to extend freshness, in a dark place at room temperature for up to 1 week, in the refrigerator for up to 2 weeks, or in the freezer for up to 6 months.

Buffalo meat is naturally quite lean and therefore great for jerky. I also love to use these classic hunter's spices with elk jerky, which is harder to source (unless you're a hunter). If you do use wild game, be especially careful. Use only game meat that has been frozen to –4°F [–15°C] for at least 4 days before proceeding with this recipe. And if grinding the meat yourself, by all means follow the directions for North African–Spiced Lamb Jerky (page 118). The directions here are for ready-ground buffalo meat because it's what is most commonly found at the meat counter for these specialty meats. Ground-meat jerkies like this one are simplest to shape with a jerky gun (see page 16). If you do not have a jerky gun, you can approximate the strips by using a pastry bag with a wide, flat tip, or by pressing the meat into 2-by-4-in [5-by-10-cm] strips with the back of a spoon.

BUFFALO JERKY WITH GIN BOTANICALS

MAKES ABOUT 1 LB [455 G]

6 juniper berries

3½ tsp kosher salt

¼ tsp freshly ground black pepper

¼ tsp ground cloves

2 lb [910 g] ground buffalo, elk, or lean beef

2 bay leaves

1 tsp minced garlic

1 Tbsp olive oil

¼ cup [60 ml] gin

1. The night before drying the meat, use a spice grinder or a mortar and pestle to grind or crush the juniper berries and ½ tsp of the salt into a coarse powder. In a small bowl, mix the juniper powder together with the remaining 3 tsp salt, the pepper, and cloves.

2. In a medium bowl, mix the ground meat, bay leaves, garlic, olive oil, and gin together with the spice mixture. Cover and refrigerate overnight.

3. Line dehydrator trays with non-stick mesh sheets that have been lightly coated with cooking oil.

4. Remove the bay leaves from the meat mixture and discard. Mix the meat mixture one more time.

5. Pipe the meat mixture in 2-by-4-in [5-by-10-cm] strips about ⅛ in [3 mm] thick onto the prepared trays. It is helpful to use a butter knife to neatly trim off the end of each meat strip. **Dry at 160° to 165°F [71° to 74°C] for 4 to 6 hours**, blotting occasionally with paper towels, until dry to the touch, not pink in the middle, and still a bit pliable. Remove from the dehydrator and blot again thoroughly with paper towels. Let cool completely.

6. Store in an airtight container, preferably with a silica gel packet to extend freshness, in a dark place at room temperature for up to 3 days, in the refrigerator for up to 1 week, or in the freezer for up to 6 months.

If there's a seasoning combination I hope to enjoy for the rest of my life, it's the warm spices used across North Africa: Pungent cumin, lemony coriander, sweet anise-like fennel seeds, and a warm touch of chile heat. Here, I mince lean leg of lamb in the food processor to make a chewy, almost sausage-like jerky. It's an unexpectedly complex taste to encounter in jerky. To make jerky strips out of ground meat, using a jerky gun is easiest, but see the headnote for Buffalo Jerky with Gin Botanicals (page 117) for alternatives.

NORTH AFRICAN– SPICED LAMB JERKY

MAKES ABOUT 1 LB [455 G]

2 lb [910 g] lamb leg, fat trimmed, cut into small chunks

1 Tbsp cumin seeds

1 tsp coriander seeds

1 tsp red pepper flakes

½ tsp fennel seeds

¼ tsp smoked paprika

¼ tsp ground cinnamon

4 tsp kosher salt

2 garlic cloves, peeled and minced

1 Tbsp olive oil

1. Put the lamb in the freezer for about 1 hour to firm up.

2. In a dry skillet over medium heat, combine the cumin seeds, coriander seeds, red pepper flakes, and fennel seeds. Cook until the cumin seeds have darkened a shade and are toasted, 30 to 60 seconds. Let cool completely.

3. In a spice grinder or mortar and pestle, pulverize the toasted spices into a fine powder. In a small bowl, stir together with the smoked paprika, cinnamon, and salt.

4. Grind the lamb using the fine blade of a meat grinder, or by pulsing it in a food processor (work in batches if you are using a food processor). In a medium bowl, mix the ground lamb with the spice mixture, garlic, and olive oil. Cover and refrigerate overnight.

5. Line dehydrator trays with non-stick mesh sheets that have been lightly coated with cooking oil.

6. Pipe the meat mixture in 2-by-4-in [5-by-10-cm] strips about ⅛ in [3 mm] thick onto the prepared trays. It is helpful to use a butter knife to neatly trim off the end of each meat strip. **Dry at 160° to 165°F [71° to 74°C] for 4 to 6 hours**, until dry to the touch, not pink in the middle, and still a bit pliable. Flip the strips once and rotate the trays once or twice during drying. Remove from the dehydrator and wrap the jerky strips in paper towels to absorb any excess fat. Let cool completely.

7. Store in an airtight container, preferably with a silica gel packet to extend freshness, in a dark place at room temperature for up to 3 days, in the refrigerator for up to 1 week, or in the freezer for up to 6 months.

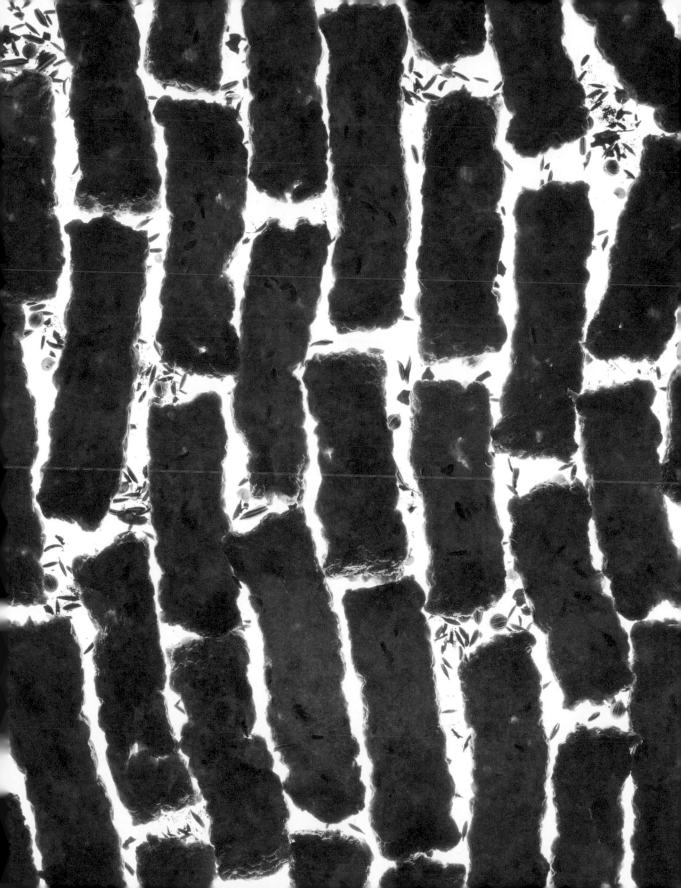

I haven't been to Malaysia, but I have been to Richmond, British Columbia, near Vancouver, where you can get almost any delicious kind of Asian snack you could desire, including Malaysian pork jerky, sweet with soy, flavored with fish sauce, and carefully grilled on special steel grates over a low charcoal fire. I decided to try my own hand at the delicious concoction in my dehydrator. Don't use pre-packaged ground pork from your local butcher; it typically contains a lot of fat and you'll want the leanest possible meat, like pork tenderloin. It's easy to mince in the food processor—or you might ask a trusted butcher to finely grind it for you. While I give instructions for drying like other jerkies, I also offer an alternative. For a little fresh-from-the-grill flavor, throw some of the almost-finished jerky under the broiler for a minute or two until the sugar in the jerky starts to caramelize. To make jerky strips out of ground meat, using a jerky gun is easiest, but see the headnote for Buffalo Jerky with Gin Botanicals (page 117) for alternatives.

MALAYSIAN-STYLE PORK JERKY

MAKES ABOUT 1¼ LB [570 G]

2½ lb [1.2 kg] pork tenderloin, fat and silver skin trimmed, and cut into 1-in [2.5-cm] chunks

¼ cup [60 ml] Shaoxing wine (Chinese rice wine) or off-dry white wine like Riesling

¼ cup [60 ml] fish sauce

½ cup [100 g] sugar

3 Tbsp soy sauce

2 garlic cloves, peeled and minced

½ tsp red pepper flakes, or to taste

1 Tbsp kosher salt

1. In a food processor, combine the pork, wine, fish sauce, sugar, soy sauce, garlic, red pepper flakes, and salt. (If you have a small machine, you may need to work in batches.) Pulse in 5-second intervals, occasionally scraping down the bowl, until the meat is finely and evenly minced. Scrape the minced pork mixture into a medium bowl, cover, and refrigerate overnight.

2. Line dehydrator trays with non-stick mesh sheets that have been lightly coated with cooking oil. (If you are going to grill or broil the jerky, cover each tray with a nonstick fruit-leather sheet instead).

3. Pipe the meat mixture in 2-by-4-in [5-by-10-cm] strips about ⅛ in [3 mm] thick onto the prepared trays. It is helpful to use a butter knife to neatly trim off the end of each meat strip. **Dry at 160° to 165°F [71° to 74°C] for 4 to 6 hours**, blotting occasionally with paper towels, until dry to the touch but still a bit pliable. (If you are planning to broil the jerky and have used fruit-leather sheets on the trays, the bottom of the jerky will be cooked but not dry; it will finish drying and also brown up in the oven.)

4. If you like, place a rack in the top of the oven and pre-heat the broiler. Remove the jerky from the dehydrator and place the jerky pale-side up on the broiler tray. Broil until the edges of the jerky turn caramel brown. You may need to work in batches. Let cool completely.

5. Store in an airtight container, preferably with a silica gel packet to extend freshness, in a dark place at room temperature for up to 3 days, in the refrigerator for up to 1 week, or in the freezer for up to 6 months.

This recipe was my attempt to make the fluffy dried pork product called pork floss (also meat wool or *bah-sang*) popular in China and Taiwan, which is dried pork that simulates the texture of cotton candy and is used as a meaty condiment to bring depth to any number of comfort foods from rice porridge (congee) to stir-fried tofu to noodles—in fact, I've taken to calling it magic noodle powder. I couldn't quite duplicate the airy texture of the commercial product; instead, the pork dries into short crunchy shards. I found that I liked the pork best in a coarse powder, and that's what I recommend you try to make. This recipe is basically dehydrated Hunan-style red-cooked pork. Feel free to enjoy some of the pork stew as you make it, drying any leftovers.

SHREDDED PORK JERKY

MAKES ABOUT 8 OZ [230 G]

2 lb [910 g] trimmed pork shoulder, cubed

2 Tbsp brown sugar

2 Tbsp vegetable oil

4 garlic cloves, peeled

3 star anise

3 green onions, white and light green parts, trimmed and sliced

2 Tbsp soy sauce

1½ cups [360 ml] low-sodium chicken stock or water

1. Blot the pork cubes with a paper towel. In a large saucepan over medium heat, combine the brown sugar and vegetable oil, stirring until the sugar has melted a bit. Add the pork and brown, stirring occasionally, for 5 to 7 minutes.

2. Add the garlic, star anise, green onions, soy sauce, and stock to the pan. Bring to a boil, turn the heat to low so the mixture simmers, and cover the pot. Skim any grayish foam off the surface of the liquid, and cook the meat until a sample cube can be easily pulled into shreds with two forks, about 1 hour and 45 minutes. Drain the pork, lay it out on a large plate, and refrigerate until it is easy to handle. When cool, shred the pork with two forks, removing any big chunks of fat.

3. Line dehydrator trays with nonstick mesh sheets that have been lightly coated with cooking oil. Line the bottom of the dehydrator with a nonstick mesh sheet for easier cleanup.

4. Lay out the pork on the prepared trays. **Dry at 165° to 170°F [74° to 77°C] for 8 to 10 hours,** blotting occasionally with paper towels, until crispy. When dry, lay the dried pork on paper towels to blot further. Let cool completely. You can keep the meat in shards or, using a food processor (or blender), grind the pork shards into a coarse powder.

5. Store in an airtight container, preferably with a silica gel packet to extend freshness, in a dark place for up to 1 week, in the refrigerator for up to 2 weeks, or in the freezer for up to 6 months.

Turkey will get firmer than other meats in the dehydrator, so this jerky truly earns its name. You might be surprised at the richness of flavor imparted by the sage and garlic marinade used here. It's a little Italian by way of the American South, thanks to a sweet touch of molasses, which plays an interesting role. Though the meat is fully cooked on the highest setting of the dehydrator, it tends to look a little pale; the molasses gives the meat an earthy sweetness and an attractive jerky shade as well.

GARLIC-SAGE TURKEY JERKY

MAKES ABOUT 1 LB [455 G]

2¼ lb [1.1 kg] turkey breast

2 Tbsp olive oil

3 garlic cloves, peeled and sliced

8 sage leaves

2 Tbsp molasses

¼ tsp freshly ground black pepper

2½ tsp kosher salt

1. Remove the skin from the turkey breast and put the breast in the freezer for 2 to 4 hours, until it is firm but not frozen solid. Cut the meat diagonally across the grain into ⅛-in [3-mm] slices. Cut any large slices into 2-in- [5-cm-] wide strips.

2. In a small saucepan over medium heat, warm the olive oil. Add the garlic and sage and cook for 1 to 2 minutes, until fragrant. Stir in the molasses and pepper, remove from the heat, and let cool to room temperature.

3. In a large bowl, toss the turkey slices with the salt and the molasses mixture, making sure all the slices are evenly coated. Cover and refrigerate overnight.

4. Line dehydrator trays with non-stick mesh sheets that have been lightly coated with cooking oil.

5. Lay out the turkey slices on the prepared trays. **Dry at 160° to 165°F [71° to 74°C] for 3 to 5 hours,** blotting occasionally with paper towels, until very dry to the touch but still a bit pliable. Let cool completely.

6. Store in an airtight container, preferably with a silica gel packet to extend freshness, in a dark place at room temperature for up to 1 week, in the refrigerator for up to 2 weeks, or in the freezer for up to 6 months.

Here in the Pacific Northwest, semidried, smoked "salmon candy" is a popular snack. You'll find it in specialty food shops and little coastal convenience stores. I relish the deep-down chew of the salmon candy, but I don't like quite so much sweetness since it masks the flavor of the fresh salmon. This recipe is my take, with maple syrup rather than brown sugar, and a pinch of paprika to lend a smoky taste without the hours of smoking. Look for sockeye or silver (coho) salmon for this recipe—they're less fatty than the majorly expensive king or Chinook salmon and work better for dried recipes.

SMOKY MAPLE SALMON JERKY

MAKES ABOUT ⅔ LB [320 G]

1½ lb [680 g] sockeye or silver salmon fillet

½ cup [120 ml] soy sauce

¼ cup [60 ml] maple syrup

½ tsp freshly ground black pepper

1 tsp smoked paprika

1. Remove the pin bones from the salmon with a pair of tweezers or pliers. (To find the bones, run your fingers along the ridge of the fillet from the head end to the tail. The flexible pin bones are lined up in a row.) Trim off any other bones near the belly area of the fish. Starting at the head end of the fillet, use a very sharp knife to cut the fish on the bias into ¼-in- [6-mm-] thick slices. Put in a large bowl and refrigerate while mixing the marinade.

2. In a small bowl, whisk together the soy sauce, maple syrup, pepper, and paprika. Pour the mixture over the salmon slices and gently toss to coat. Let marinate for 3 hours, and then drain the fish thoroughly. If not drying right away, put the drained salmon slices on a plate, cover, and refrigerate for up to 12 hours.

3. Line dehydrator trays with nonstick mesh sheets that have been lightly coated with cooking oil.

4. Lay out the salmon on the prepared trays. **Dry at 160° to 165°F [71° to 74°C] for 3 to 5 hours**, blotting occasionally with paper towels, until dry and leathery to the touch and chewy. Let cool completely.

5. Store in an airtight container, preferably with a silica gel packet to extend freshness, in the refrigerator for up to 2 weeks, or in the freezer for up to 6 months.

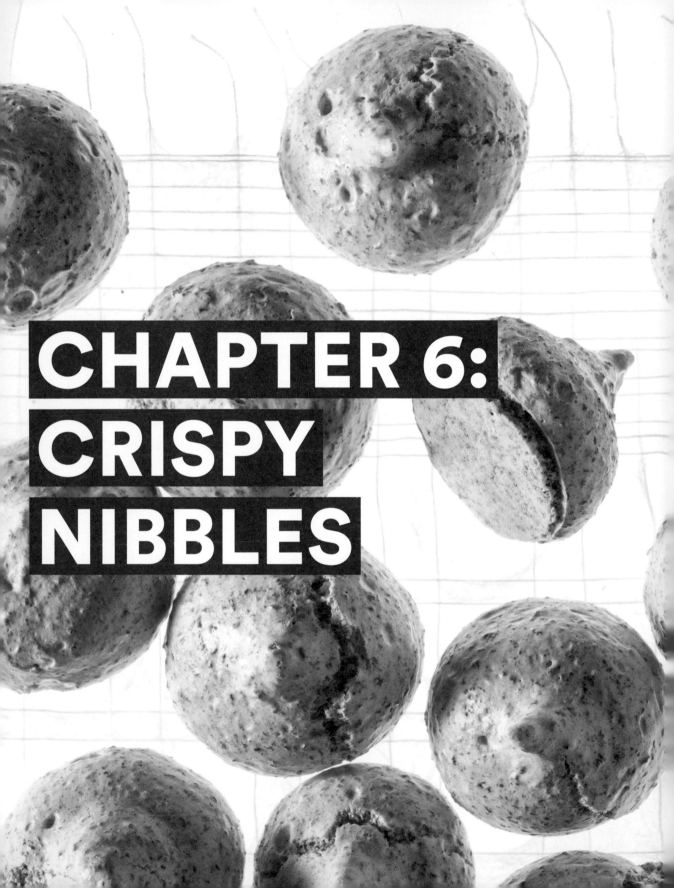

CHAPTER 6: CRISPY NIBBLES

I first started thinking about the dehydrator as a tool for making snacks and sweets when I looked over René Redzepi's *Noma: Time and Place in Nordic Cuisine*, his first, beautiful cookbook. Throughout the book, he showed meringues, some sweet, some savory, to add sculptural punctuation on his dishes. When I reviewed the recipes, I realized he used a dehydrator, not an oven, to get perfectly dry, airy meringues.

The dehydrator is often a great choice for preparations like meringues that might otherwise call for a low-temperature oven. Because the heat generally stays below browning levels in a dehydrator, you can maximize dryness—that is, crispy crackly airiness—without worrying about burning your ingredients. In other words, even if you're not a world-renowned chef like Redzepi, the dehydrator can be a perfect snack machine, making not just meringues but croutons and pita chips that are shatteringly crisp, gluten-free flax crackers for dipping or nibbling on their own, and slightly sweet granola and other breakfast cereals made with and without grains.

Sometimes I have a hard time getting my granola as consistently crunchy and clumpy as I like. In the oven, sometimes the coconut burns while the oat flakes are still a little moist. In the dehydrator, however, you can leave granola drying at a temperature low enough to avoid any bitter browning. Making granola in a dehydrator also means that you might want to pre-toast some of the components before you dry them. So I lightly brown ingredients like coconut and sliced almonds in a skillet so that the flavor is rich and developed.

This chapter is filled with ideas for highly satisfying nibbles, both sweet and savory.

In my world, a crouton should always be homemade. Sometimes, with, say, a very smooth soup, a neat little toasted cube of white bread is called for, but more often I like my croutons craggy, tasty, and as charismatic as possible. These mustard-kissed rye croutons fit the bill. Since they aren't reclusive, serve them in strong company. Sprinkle them atop a hearty beet soup, or toss them in a rustic salad of robust chicories. If some warm bacon or duck confit were to fall in the salad bowl, so much the better. A word of salad-saucing advice: Start with the croutons. Dress them lightly first on their own, then, afterward, toss in the rest of the salad ingredients, adding more vinaigrette if needed.

MUSTARD RYE CROUTONS

MAKES ABOUT 6 CUPS [280 G]

1-lb [455-g] loaf rye bread

1 small garlic clove, peeled and minced

2 Tbsp olive oil

1 Tbsp Dijon mustard

Fine sea salt

1. If you are working with an unsliced loaf, cut the loaf in half lengthwise, and pull out chunks of bread approximately ½ to 1 in [12 mm to 2.5 cm] across, leaving the crust behind. (The crust is delicious for bread crumbs. Dry it at the same time as the croutons, and then grind it in a food processor.) If you are working with sliced bread, pull the crust off and tear each slice into pieces as described.

2. In a large bowl, whisk together the garlic, olive oil, and mustard. Add the torn bread and toss thoroughly to coat evenly. Sprinkle in 1 tsp salt and toss well to distribute. Taste and add more salt, if desired.

3. Lay out the torn bread on the dehydrator trays. (There's no need to line the trays, because the bread is big enough to not fall through standard tray holes and it's not sticky.) **Dry at 160° to 165°F [71° to 74°C] for 3 to 4 hours**, until the croutons are completely dry. Let cool completely.

4. Store in an airtight container, preferably with a silica gel packet to extend freshness, in a dark place at room temperature for up to 1 week. Near the end of that storage time, you may want to freshen the croutons in the dehydrator for about 1 hour before serving.

If you are getting ready for a party, sometimes nothing is more helpful than freeing up some oven space. The dehydrator allows you to produce flavorful baguette crisps to go with cheese or to use as the basis for hors d'oeuvres. Here, I make up for a lack of toasting in the dehydrator by browning the butter that is brushed on bread slices before drying. For a delicious finished recipe using these croutons, see Crackly Thyme Crostini with Goat Cheese, Peppers, and Olives (page 130).

THYME-SCENTED CROSTINI

MAKES ABOUT 50 CROSTINI

1 baguette, cut diagonally into ¼-in [6-mm] slices

½ cup [110 g] unsalted butter

3 or 4 sprigs thyme

1 garlic clove, peeled and halved

Fine sea salt

1. Lay out the baguette slices on the dehydrator trays. (There's no need to line the trays, because the bread is big enough to not fall through standard tray holes and it's not sticky.)

2. In a small saucepan over medium heat, melt the butter with the thyme and garlic. Cook for 3 to 4 minutes, until the butter solids turn a light almond brown. Pour the melted butter into a small bowl. Discard the thyme sprigs.

3. Using a pastry brush, paint the top of each baguette slice with a light coat of the melted browned butter. Season each bread slice with a bit of salt.

4. Dry the bread slices at 160° to 165°F [71° to 74°C] for 3 to 4 hours, until completely crisp and dry. Let cool completely.

5. Store in an airtight container, preferably with a silica gel packet to extend freshness, in a dark place at room temperature for up to 1 week. Near the end of that storage time, you may want to freshen the crostini in the dehydrator for 30 minutes before serving.

This recipe combines many elements of the dehydrator repertoire: the chewy intensity of dried roasted red bell peppers, reconstituted and marinated in olive oil; the crisp perfection of dried brown-butter crostini; and the unexpected crunch and salinity of dried olives. Any one of these elements tastes wonderful on its own, but when combined, you have something delightful.

CRACKLY THYME CROSTINI WITH GOAT CHEESE, PEPPERS, AND OLIVES

SERVES 12 TO 15

4 Dried Roasted Red Bell Peppers (page 108)

1 tsp balsamic vinegar

1 shallot, peeled and finely minced

½ cup [120 ml] olive oil, plus more for drizzling

2 Tbsp minced Italian flat-leaf parsley leaves

Fine sea salt

4 oz [115 g] fresh goat cheese (chèvre)

1 recipe Thyme-Scented Crostini (page 129)

2 Tbsp Dried Black Olive Crumble (page 31)

1. In a small bowl, pour hot water over the dried bell peppers and let sit for 20 minutes to soften. In another small bowl, pour the vinegar over the shallot and marinate for 15 minutes to soften a bit.

2. When the peppers are tender, drain and slice them into ribbons. Toss with the marinated shallot. Stir in the olive oil and parsley, and season with salt. (This marinade can be refrigerated for 24 hours before serving. Let it come to room temperature before assembling the crostini.)

3. Spread a thin layer of goat cheese across each crostino. Spoon some slivers of the bell pepper marinade atop the cheese, drizzling some of the marinade oil onto the bread as well. Top each crostino with a pinch of olive crumble. Serve immediately.

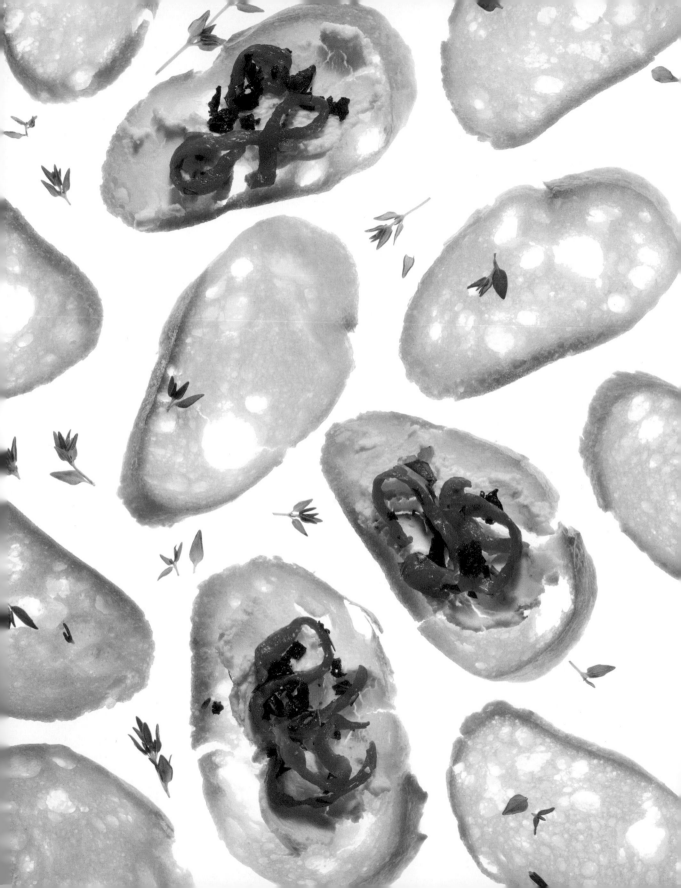

With the deli-delicious flavor of caraway seeds and a bit of mustard, these crackers are a blast to make. You spread the gelatinous mixture of flaxseed and chia seeds thinly on a nonstick sheet, and after it is dried, the mixture crisps into a thin wafer, with edges that curl up dramatically off the surface. To serve, simply crack the large wafer into generous shards to dip into hummus, serve alongside cheese, or snack on like chips. These crackers are best if eaten within 3 days of drying.

CARAWAY-FLAX CRACKERS

MAKES 8 TO 10 SNACK SERVINGS

½ cup [70 g] flaxseed

¼ cup [35 g] chia seeds

1 tsp caraway seeds

1 tsp fine sea salt

¼ tsp freshly ground black pepper

1 tsp Dijon mustard

1 Tbsp potato starch

1½ cups [360 ml] water

1. Line dehydrator trays with nonstick fruit-leather sheets.

2. In a dry skillet over medium heat, toast the flaxseed for 1 to 2 minutes, until the seeds start to toast and a few seeds pop. Transfer to a medium mixing bowl. Add the chia seeds, caraway seeds, salt, pepper, mustard, potato starch, and water to the bowl and stir to combine. Cover and let sit at room temperature for 1 to 4 hours; the seeds will form a gummy gel.

3. Using an offset spatula or the back of a spoon, spread the seed mixture thinly on the prepared trays. Do not worry about geometric perfection; these crackers should have organic shapes. **Dry at 135°F [57°F] for 6 to 8 hours,** until completely dry on the top and bottom. Gently flip the large crackers midway through drying. Let cool completely, then break the crackers into large shards.

4. Store in an airtight container, preferably with a silica gel packet to extend freshness, in a dark place at room temperature for up to 1 week.

Pita chips are the perfect dipping vehicle for the vibrant dips of the Mediterranean, like baba ghanoush, tzatziki, and, of course, hummus. Here, they're topped by a Middle Eastern seasoning mixture called *za'atar*, which usually contains za'atar, a cousin to oregano, plus lemony sumac, sesame seeds, salt, and sometimes other spices like cumin or marjoram. Look for za'atar at Middle Eastern specialty stores or online at www.worldspice.com. Or you can make your own za'atar-inspired blend by stirring together 2 Tbsp dried thyme, 2 Tbsp sesame seeds, 2 tsp sumac, and ½ tsp fine sea salt. The spice mixture makes a zingy, tart-savory snack out of leftover pita bread, perfect for dipping or tossing with a cucumber and tomato salad for a variation of the Middle Eastern bread salad known as fattoush. The chips themselves couldn't be simpler to make.

ZA'ATAR PITA CHIPS

MAKES 6 TO 8 SNACK SERVINGS

Four 6-in [15-cm] whole-wheat pita rounds, each cut into 10 wedges

2 Tbsp olive oil

1 Tbsp za'atar

½ tsp fine sea salt

1. In a large bowl, toss the pita wedges with the olive oil to evenly coat. Sprinkle in the za'atar and salt, and toss again to evenly distribute the spices.

2. Lay out the pita wedges on the dehydrator trays. (There's no need to line the trays, because the wedges are big enough to not fall through standard tray holes and they're not sticky.) **Dry at 160° to 165°F [71° to 74°C] for 3 to 4 hours**, until very crisp. Let cool completely.

3. Store in an airtight container, preferably with a silica gel packet to extend freshness, in a dark place at room temperature for up to 2 weeks.

When you put bananas together with brown sugar, something magical happens beyond just sweetness; the bananas become warmer in tone, almost spicier, and, in my opinion, much more compelling. And combining them with toasted pecans adds wonderful snap and flavor to a simple trail mix. The drying time for sugared bananas is a bit longer than for plain ones, because there's added sugar (see Judging Doneness, page 19). To minimize sticky spots on the bananas, you may choose to condition the bananas before mixing with the nuts.

BANANAS FOSTER TRAIL MIX

MAKES ABOUT 2 CUPS [85 G]

1½ cups [360 ml] water

¼ cup [50 g] brown sugar

¼ cup [60 ml] dark rum

5 ripe, unblemished bananas, peeled and cut into ¼-in- [6-mm-] thick slices

⅔ cup [70 g] whole pecans

1. Line dehydrator trays with non-stick mesh sheets that have been lightly coated with cooking oil.

2. In a medium saucepan over medium-high heat, combine ¼ cup [60 ml] of the water and the brown sugar and bring to a boil, stirring, until the sugar has melted. Whisk in the rum and remaining 1¼ cups [300 ml] water. Toss the banana slices with the mixture, remove from the heat, and let sit for 10 to 15 minutes. Drain the banana slices.

3. Lay out the banana slices on the prepared trays. **Dry at 135°F [57°C] for 14 to 18 hours**, until chewy, a bit leathery, and no longer squishy inside. Let cool completely. You may choose to condition the bananas at this point (see page 21).

4. Preheat the oven to 300°F [150°C].

5. Spread the pecans on a baking sheet and toast until they are slightly darkened at their interior (break one open to check doneness), 12 to 15 minutes. Let cool completely.

6. Mix together the toasted pecans and dried banana slices.

7. Store in an airtight container, preferably with a silica gel packet to extend freshness, in a dark place at room temperature for up to 2 weeks.

Granola might be too limiting a name for this snackable mixture. Perched between savory and sweet, it is so full of flavor and crunch that you will find yourself spooning it up to add to your breakfast yogurt, topping salads with it, snacking on it midafternoon, and topping your ice cream with it in the evening. It's grain-free to please your Paleo friends, tree-nut free for friends with allergies, and, if your vegan friends come over, you could use egg replacer to bind the seeds and agave in place of the egg white and honey.

SEEDY NO-GRAIN GRANOLA

MAKES ABOUT 3½ CUPS [220 G]

½ cup [65 g] pepitas (shelled pumpkin seeds)

¼ cup [30 g] sunflower seeds, shelled

½ cup [70 g] flaxseed

½ cup [70 g] chia seeds

1 tsp ground cinnamon

½ tsp salt

Scant ⅛ tsp ground cloves

2 Tbsp honey

1 egg white, beaten until frothy

1. Line dehydrator trays with nonstick fruit-leather sheets.

2. In a dry skillet over medium-high heat, warm the pepitas, stirring occasionally. When the seeds start to crackle and snap vigorously, after 2 to 4 minutes, pour onto a baking sheet.

3. Heat the sunflower seeds in the dry skillet over medium-high heat, stirring occasionally. When the seeds color slightly and occasionally pop, after about 1 minute, pour onto the baking sheet.

4. Toast the flaxseed in the dry skillet over medium heat. When they start to pop vigorously, 30 seconds to 1 minute, pour onto the baking sheet.

5. Finally, heat the chia seeds in the dry skillet over medium heat until they color slightly, about 1 minute (they will not pop as much as the other seeds). Pour onto the baking sheet. Let cool completely.

6. Pour all the seeds into a large bowl and add the cinnamon, salt, and cloves. Whisk the honey vigorously into the egg white and pour into the seed mixture. Stir with a wooden spoon to evenly distribute the egg mixture throughout the seeds.

7. Pour the seed mixture onto the prepared trays. Press it into a very thin, even layer. **Dry at 160° to 165°F [71° to 74°C] for 4 to 6 hours**, until the granola is dry to the touch on the top and bottom surfaces and crunchy. Let cool completely. Break into small chunks.

8. Store in an airtight container, preferably with a silica gel packet to extend freshness, in a dark place at room temperature for up to 2 weeks.

In this recipe, I use a bit of condensed milk—the secret to dulce de leche—to add sweetness and richness to a granola that's as much a dessert as it is a whole-grain, wholesome snack.

SPICED DULCE DE LECHE GRANOLA

MAKES ABOUT 4¾ CUPS [465 G]

½ cup [30 g] unsweetened coconut flakes (the wide kind, often called coconut chips)

½ cup [60 g] sliced almonds

3 cups [250 g] rolled oats (not quick cooking)

¼ tsp ground cinnamon

¼ tsp ground cardamom

Fine sea salt

¼ cup [50 g] coconut oil

1 Tbsp unsalted butter

¼ cup [60 ml] canned condensed milk

2 Tbsp brown sugar

2 egg whites

1. Line the dehydrator trays with nonstick fruit-leather sheets.

2. In a large skillet over medium heat, toast the coconut, stirring occasionally, until the edges of the flakes take on a golden straw color. Transfer to a large bowl and wipe out the pan. Put the almonds in the skillet and toast until the edges of the slices take on a light golden brown color. Transfer to the bowl with the coconut. Add the oats, cinnamon, cardamom, and ½ tsp salt to the bowl and stir to mix.

3. In a small saucepan over medium heat, combine the coconut oil, butter, condensed milk, and brown sugar and heat, stirring occasionally, until the coconut oil is melted and the brown sugar has dissolved. The condensed milk may congeal and look a bit fudgy in texture, which is okay. Pour the hot mixture into the oat mixture and stir well to combine. Once the mixture is cool enough to touch, you may find your hands work best for combining the sweet mixture.

4. In a small bowl, whisk the egg whites until frothy, and then pour into the oat mixture. Fold to thoroughly distribute the egg whites.

5. Lay out the granola on the prepared trays. Spread the mixture into a thin layer, pressing down firmly on top and on the sides to compact it (which will help develop big clumps). **Dry at 160°F [71°C] for 4 to 6 hours,** turning with a spatula after 3 hours (keeping it in large pieces if possible), until very dry and crunchy. Let cool completely.

6. Store in an airtight container, preferably with a silica gel packet to extend freshness, in a dark place at room temperature for up to 2 weeks.

Muesli, a Swiss morning classic combination of oats, nuts, seeds, and fruit, most traditionally is served as a cold porridge after a night of soaking in yogurt. But today, the term can also function more broadly as a restrained cousin to granola. Traditional muesli is an untoasted mixture, but in this case, I burnished a very lightly sweetened combination of toasted rye and oat flakes, almonds, and coconut in the oven and then set off the nutty cereal with the dark ruby tanginess of dried strawberry slices. My daughter likes this cereal as an after-school snack—if she lets it soak for a little while, the milk takes on a distinctly delicious strawberry flavor. It's reminiscent of the strawberry milk powder of my childhood, without the food coloring or the copious sugar.

If you have previously dried strawberries in your pantry, use ½ cup [35 g] of them in place of the fresh strawberries in this recipe.

STRAWBERRY-COCONUT MUESLI

MAKES 4 CUPS [390 G]

1 pt [340 g] fresh strawberries, stemmed and cut into ⅛-in [3-mm] slices

1½ cup [135 g] rye flakes

1½ cup [125 g] rolled oats (not quick cooking)

2 Tbsp agave syrup

2 Tbsp coconut oil, melted

¾ tsp fine sea salt

½ cup [60 g] almonds

½ cup [30 g] unsweetened coconut flakes (the wide kind, also known as coconut chips)

1. Line dehydrator trays with non-stick mesh sheets that have been lightly coated with cooking oil.

2. Lay out the strawberry slices on the prepared trays. **Dry at 135°F [57°C] for 8 to 12 hours,** until fully dry to the touch and leathery-crisp. Let cool completely.

3. Preheat the oven to 325°F [165°C].

4. In a large bowl, mix the rye flakes and oats with the agave syrup, coconut oil, and salt. Toss well to ensure even distribution of the ingredients. Lay out the mixture in a thin layer on a rimmed baking sheet. Bake for 16 to 18 minutes, until the rye and oats are lightly toasted. Let cool completely.

5. Lay out the almonds on a baking sheet and toast in the oven until the nuts are warm through and lightly browned at their centers, 12 to 14 minutes. Let cool completely, and then chop the almonds roughly.

6. Lay out the coconut flakes on a baking sheet and toast in the oven for 8 to 10 minutes, until the coconut is lightly browned on the edges. Let cool completely.

7. In a large bowl, mix together the rye-oatmeal mixture, chopped almonds, toasted coconut, and the dried strawberries.

8. Store in an airtight container, preferably with a silica gel packet to extend freshness, in a dark place at room temperature for up to 2 weeks.

Oven-cooked meringues have crackly, sometimes lightly browned crusts and interiors that are chewy, maybe even a little damp. Dehydrator meringues are different. These little cookies emerge snowy-hued, airy, and crisp all the way through, and they last for a very long time. This mixture can be piped into thin letters or hearts, or you can dollop it into nests for a Pavlova, the elegant dessert of meringue topped with whipped cream and berries. I use an Italian meringue base that sets the egg whites with a hot sugar syrup. You'll need a candy thermometer for making this. Choose a warm, dry day for making meringues (whether in a regular oven or a dehydrator). They have a hard time getting truly crisp on a humid day.

VANILLA MERINGUES

MAKES ABOUT 30 MERINGUES

3 egg whites, at
room temperature

Pinch of salt

1 tsp white wine vinegar

¾ cup [150 g] superfine sugar

¼ cup [60 ml] water

1 Tbsp light corn syrup

1 tsp vanilla extract

1. Line dehydrator trays with nonstick fruit-leather sheets.

2. Put the egg whites in the bowl of a stand mixer fitted with the whisk attachment (or in a medium bowl with a hand mixer). Mix on medium-high speed until foamy. Add the salt and vinegar and continue to whisk to soft peaks. Turn off the mixer.

3. In a small saucepan over medium-high heat, combine the sugar, water, and corn syrup. Whisk until the sugar has melted, then leave undisturbed until the syrup reaches 248°F [120°C] on a candy thermometer. Remove from the heat and let cool to 240°F [116°C].

4. Start the stand mixer (or hand mixer) on medium speed and, working carefully, slowly pour the hot syrup into the mixer bowl in a thin stream, avoiding both the side of the bowl and the whisk. Once the syrup has been mixed in, add the vanilla and mix for 30 seconds. Then, turn the mixer to high speed and whisk the mixture until the bottom of the bowl cools to room temperature, about 5 minutes. The resulting meringue will be glossy and thick, like marshmallow spread.

5. Pipe or spoon the mixture onto the prepared trays in 1-Tbsp mounds. **Dry at 160° to 165°F [71° to 74°C] for 3 to 4 hours,** until the meringues are airy dry and crisp on the top and bottom. Let cool completely.

6. Store in an airtight container, preferably with a silica gel packet to extend freshness, in a dark place at room temperature for up to 2 weeks.

VARIATIONS

Shapes: Spell your child's name for a special birthday cake decoration, or top valentine tarts with pretty hearts. Use a piping bag outfitted with a plain ¼-in [3-mm] tip to pipe meringue into letters or shapes (make extras; they are delicate). Dry for 2 to 3 hours until completely crisp.

Pavlovas: Pipe or spoon the meringue into 3-in [7.5-cm] nests that are thinner at the center than the edges. Dry for 6 to 8 hours, until completely crisp. Top with vanilla ice cream, fresh berries, and whipped cream.

Stracciatella is among my kids' favorite ice cream flavors. It is vanilla gelato embedded with delicate little shavings of chocolate. Here, I've loaded the meringues with a solid dose of shaved bittersweet chocolate for an effect that is crisp and light while possessing an almost truffle-like intensity. A rasp grater, like a Microplane, is a perfect tool for preparing your chocolate shavings.

STRACCIATELLA MERINGUES

MAKES ABOUT 30 MERINGUES

3 egg whites, at room temperature

Pinch of salt

1 tsp white wine vinegar

⅔ cup [135 g] superfine sugar

¼ cup [60 ml] water

1 Tbsp corn syrup

1 tsp vanilla

3 oz [85 g] bittersweet chocolate, finely grated

1. Line dehydrator trays with nonstick fruit-leather sheets.

2. Put the egg whites in the bowl of a stand mixer fitted with the whisk attachment (or in a medium bowl with a hand mixer). Mix on medium-high speed until foamy. Add the salt and vinegar and continue to whisk to soft peaks. Turn off the mixer.

3. In a small saucepan over medium-high heat, combine the sugar, water, and corn syrup. Whisk until the sugar has melted, then leave undisturbed until the syrup reaches 248°F [120°C] on a candy thermometer. Remove from the heat and let cool to 240°F [116°C].

4. Start the stand mixer (or hand mixer) on medium speed and, working carefully, slowly pour the hot syrup into the mixer bowl in a thin stream, avoiding both the side of the bowl and the whisk. Once the syrup has been mixed in, add the vanilla and mix for 30 seconds. Then, turn the mixer to high speed and whisk the mixture until the bottom of the bowl cools to room temperature, about 5 minutes. The resulting meringue will be glossy and thick, like marshmallow spread. Fold in the chocolate shavings.

5. Pipe or spoon the mixture onto the prepared trays in 1-Tbsp mounds. **Dry at 160° to 165°F [71° to 74°C] for 4 to 6 hours,** until the meringues are airy dry and crisp on the top and bottom. Let cool completely.

6. Store in an airtight container, preferably with a silica gel packet to extend freshness, in a dark place at room temperature for up to 2 weeks.

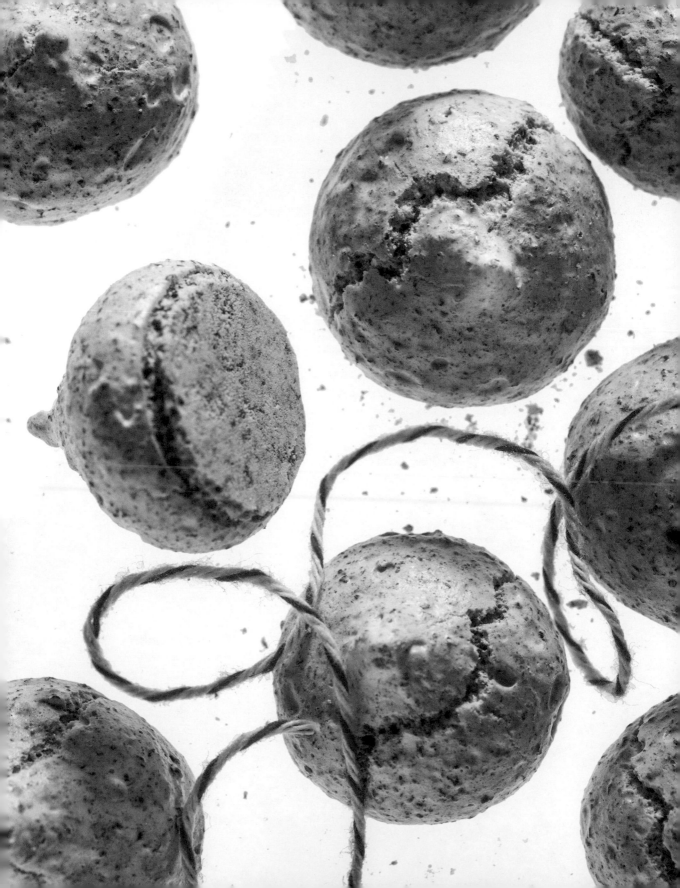

CHAPTER 7: BACKPACKING RECIPES

This chapter presents a selection of my favorite lightweight, quick-cooking food for backpackers.

I stick with basics, which can supplement purchased freeze-dried meals or fresh foods. For protein, remember that you can stir in some pieces of jerky into a soup or pilaf, and you can dry tofu or shreds of beef or chicken and stir that into your backwoods meals.

The trick to reconstituting meals that you have dried yourself is time. You won't want to waste too much firewood or cooking gas on stewing your food for long periods. So in these recipes, you pour boiling water onto the dried ingredients in a pot, cover, and let sit for 15 to 20 minutes to rehydrate before eating. The more time you allow for rehydrating, the more evenly all the little edges of the dried food will soften. Then you just pop it over the flame to heat up. Remember that cooking at high altitudes will likely require more time and more water, due to faster evaporation, than when cooking at sea level.

Beyond these recipes, your own dried ingredients also can make great add-ins for simple backpacking meals. Add some dried leeks and peas to a backcountry pasta dish; bring along some dried mushrooms, onion, and bell peppers to make the freeze-dried scrambled breakfast eggs enticing; and throw a handful of dried cranberries into your pancake mix for a welcome sweet-tart appeal. Some dried fresh produce can go a long way in making your backwoods cooking more tasty.

And don't forget those easy-to-pack flavor boosters that can make an after-hike meal so much more enjoyable. Some Umami Dust (page 30) or Herbes de Provence Salt (page 33) can add a bit of magic to a wilderness repast.

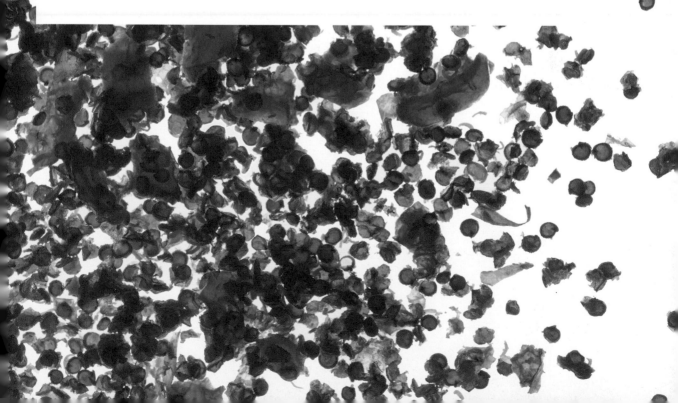

Packaged instant oatmeal is quick and easy to prepare, but it tends to be sloppy sweet and mushy. Steel-cut oats have a toothsome character, which can be so satisfying in the wilderness. And you can add big chunks of home-dried apples, giving you much more to savor when you wake up on a chilly morning on the trail.

APPLE-CINNAMON OATMEAL

MAKES ABOUT 4 SERVINGS

3 cups [710 ml] water

1 cup [160 g] Irish or Scottish steel-cut oats

¼ tsp salt

2 Tbsp brown sugar

½ tsp ground cinnamon

1 cup [20 g] chopped Dried Cinnamon Apples (page 58)

1. Line dehydrator trays with nonstick fruit-leather sheets.

2. In a medium saucepan over high heat, bring the water to a boil. Stir in the oats, salt, brown sugar, and cinnamon. Bring to a simmer, turn the heat to low, and simmer for about 20 minutes, stirring occasionally, until creamy. Remove from the heat, and let cool to lukewarm, stirring occasionally.

3. Spread out the oatmeal mixture as thinly as possible on the prepared trays. **Dry at 145°F [63°C] for 9 to 12 hours**, until crackly dry. Let cool completely.

4. In a food processor (or blender), grind the dried oatmeal into a coarse powder with a few chunks remaining for texture. Stir the dried apples into the dried oatmeal.

5. Store in an airtight container, preferably with a silica gel packet to extend freshness, in a dark place at room temperature for up to 2 weeks, or in the freezer for up to 6 months.

TO PREPARE 1 SERVING:

In a bowl, combine ¾ cup [50 g] oatmeal with ¾ cup [180 ml] boiling water. Cover, let sit for 10 minutes, then stir. Add more water if necessary for desired consistency. Serve with brown sugar or maple syrup, if desired.

I'm letting my Pacific Northwest pride show here. Come late August, it seems you can't go on a high-altitude hike in Washington without running into patches of shiny blue huckleberries. They look a lot like blueberries, but they're more tart, and have a little more depth than the plump blueberries you find at the grocery store. (They are more like East Coast low-bush blueberries.) Huckleberries taste wonderful dried, and when I don't have fresh-picked berries to work with, I put them in the dehydrator straight from the freezer (in fact, since the cell walls of frozen berries have been damaged in freezing, they tend to dry faster than pristine fresh berries). Of course, you can use dried blueberries in this recipe, if that's what's available. These pancakes rise high and have an earthy texture, thanks to the cornmeal.

BUTTERMILK-HUCKLEBERRY PANCAKE MIX

MAKES ABOUT 4 CUPS [520 G]

4 cups [460 g] fresh or frozen huckleberries or blueberries

1 cup [140 g] medium ground cornmeal

2 cups [240 g] all-purpose flour

2 tsp baking soda

2 tsp baking powder

1 cup [200 g] sifted buttermilk powder

5 Tbsp [30 g] powdered eggs or egg replacer

2 Tbsp sugar

1½ tsp fine sea salt

1. Line dehydrator trays with non-stick mesh sheets that have been lightly coated with cooking oil.

2. Pick over the berries and discard any bugs, leaves, or undesirable berries.

3. Lay out the berries on the prepared trays. **Dry at 135°F [57°C] for 10 to 12 hours from frozen, 16 to 24 hours from fresh,** until shriveled, chewy, and no longer squishy when pinched. Let cool completely.

4. In a large bowl, whisk together the cornmeal, flour, baking soda, baking powder, buttermilk powder, powdered eggs, sugar, and salt. Stir in the dried berries.

5. Store in an airtight container, preferably with a silica gel packet to extend freshness, in a dark place at room temperature for up to 2 months.

TO PREPARE 4 PANCAKES:

In a small bowl, stir together 1 cup [130 g] pancake mix and ½ cup [120 ml] water. Let rest for 10 minutes.

Heat a frying pan over medium-high heat, then add 2 tsp vegetable oil and swirl to cover the bottom of the pan. Drop in 2 Tbsp batter for each pancake, and cook until lightly browned on one side, 1½ to 2 minutes. Flip the pancake and cook for 1 minute longer, until lightly browned and puffed up. Serve with maple syrup.

Soups are a wonderful way to bring some home-cooked goodness into the woods. The trick in drying soups is to make them a bit more concentrated (using less liquid) than you normally would. In this recipe, I even use a bouillon cube to add extra rich flavor. When cooking dried soups, thin them with water to your desired consistency and flavor intensity.

EARTHY MUSHROOM SOUP

MAKES ABOUT 9 SERVINGS

2 Tbsp olive oil

2 medium onions, chopped finely

3 garlic cloves, peeled and sliced thinly

1½ lb [680 g] cremini mushrooms, trimmed, and cut into ¼-in [6-mm] slices

1 tsp fine sea salt

¼ tsp freshly ground black pepper

¼ tsp smoked paprika

1 Tbsp Umami Dust (page 30; optional)

½ cup [120 ml] dry sake or white wine

2 chicken or mushroom bouillon cubes, or 2 tsp chicken bouillon concentrate

1. Line dehydrator trays with nonstick fruit-leather sheets.

2. In a large nonreactive Dutch oven or soup pot over medium-high heat, warm the olive oil. Add the onions and cook, stirring occasionally, for about 5 minutes, until fragrant and translucent at the edges. Add the garlic and cook for 1 minute. Add the mushrooms, stirring well to coat with the onion mixture. Let cook, undisturbed, for about 5 minutes, stirring only if the mixture seems to be sticking to the bottom of the pan. Add the salt, pepper, paprika, and umami dust (if using), stirring well to distribute evenly. The mushrooms will release their juices, and then after 10 to 15 minutes that liquid should be reduced by about half, giving the mushrooms a glossy appearance. Add the sake and bouillon cubes and stir to make sure the bouillon dissolves. Cook for about 5 minutes, until the liquid is glossy once again and coats a spoon. Let cool completely.

3. Spread out the mushroom mixture in a thin, even layer on the prepared trays. **Dry at 135°F [57°C] for 18 to 24 hours**, until leathery and dry to the touch. Halfway through the drying process, peel the soup layer off the sheets and flip for the most even drying. Let cool completely, and then break up into small pieces.

4. Store in an airtight container, preferably with a silica gel packet to extend freshness, in a dark place at room temperature for up to 1 month, or in the freezer for up to 6 months.

TO PREPARE 1 SERVING:

In a small pot, stir ½ cup [40 g] dried soup mix into ⅔ cup [160 ml] boiling water. Cover and let sit for 10 minutes. Reheat to the desired temperature, adding a bit more hot water if you want a thinner consistency and a less intense flavor.

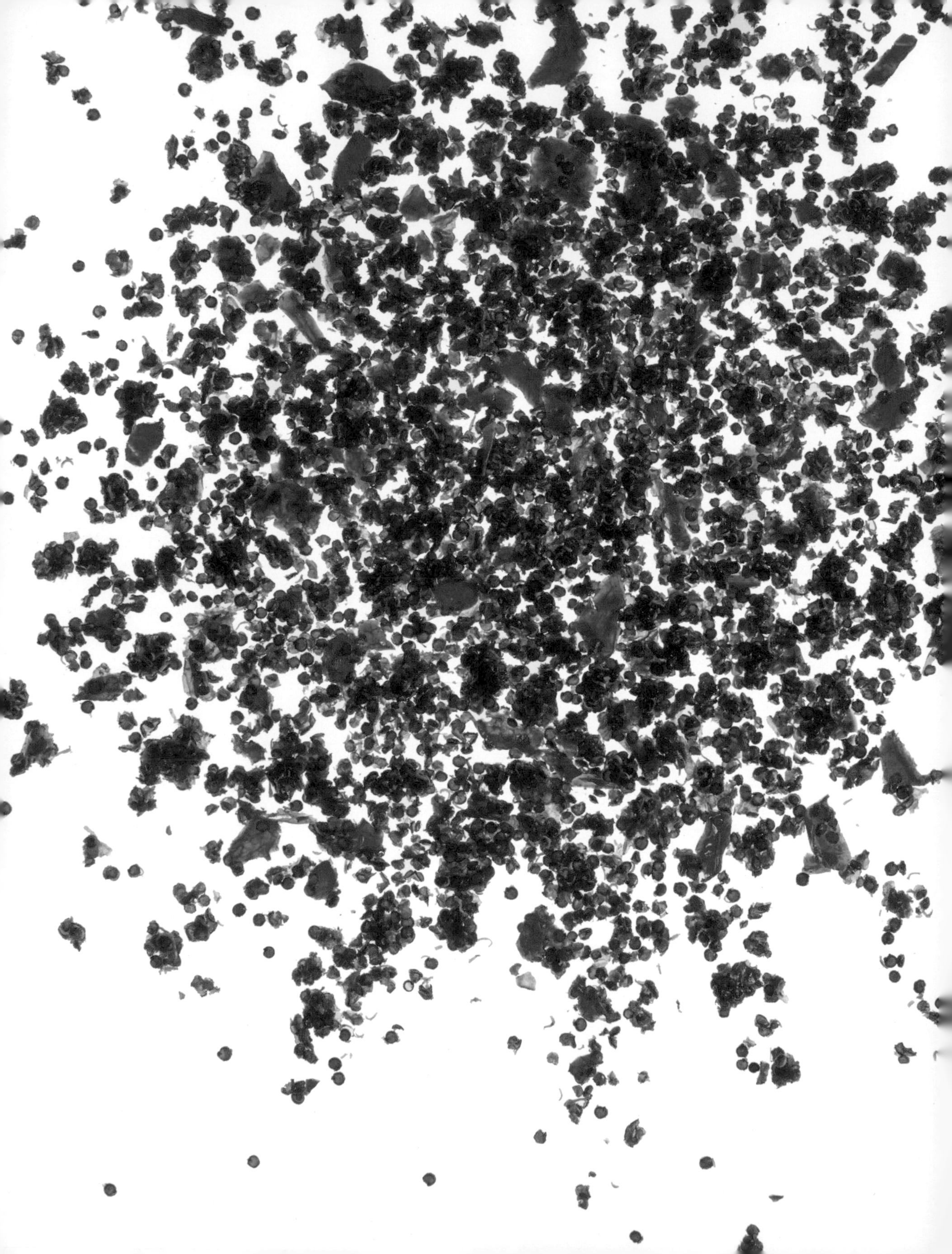

Quinoa is a great option to have on a backpacking trip, because this nutty, satisfying food is high in protein. Your stomach will be content for hours after a hearty meal built around this pilaf. It's even a tasty little snack in its dried form. Since dehydrated meals lose a bit of their toothsome quality in rehydrating, I like to compensate by packing along some chopped toasted walnuts to top off the dish. To preserve some nice texture, for this recipe, use uncooked quinoa, not the pre-cooked "quick" quinoa you might find in some stores.

RED BELL PEPPER QUINOA PILAF

MAKES 2 SERVINGS AS A MAIN COURSE, 4 AS A SIDE

2 cups [160 g] red quinoa

¼ cup [60 ml] olive oil

2 large onions, peeled and minced

1 garlic clove, peeled and minced

2 tsp tomato paste

2 red bell peppers, stemmed, seeded, and minced

1 tsp minced fresh rosemary leaves, or ¼ tsp crumbled dried rosemary leaves

Fine sea salt

1. Line dehydrator trays with nonstick fruit-leather sheets.

2. Rinse and drain the quinoa twice in cold water.

3. In a large, heavy nonreactive saucepan over medium heat, warm the olive oil. Add the onions, garlic, tomato paste, bell peppers, rosemary, and 1 tsp salt. Cook, stirring frequently, for 15 to 20 minutes, until the vegetables are tender and glossy. Add the drained quinoa, 3 cups [720 ml] water, and 1 tsp salt. Bring the mixture to a boil, cover, turn the heat to low, and simmer for 18 to 25 minutes, until the tail-like germ of the quinoa grains has unfurled and the water is fully absorbed. Taste and season with salt, if desired. Uncover, toss, and let cool to room temperature.

4. Spread out the quinoa in a thin layer on the prepared trays. **Dry at 135°F [57°C] for 6 to 8 hours,** until the quinoa mixture is fully dry and crumbly. Let cool completely.

5. Store in an airtight container, preferably with a silica gel packet to extend freshness, in a dark place at room temperature for up to 1 month, or in the freezer for up to 6 months.

TO PREPARE 1 SIDE SERVING:

In a small pot, stir ½ cup [20 g] dried quinoa pilaf into ½ cup [120 ml] boiling water. Cover and let sit for 15 to 20 minutes. Simmer the pilaf over medium heat, for 3 to 5 minutes, adding a bit more water if needed. Sprinkle the hot pilaf with toasted walnuts, if desired, before serving.

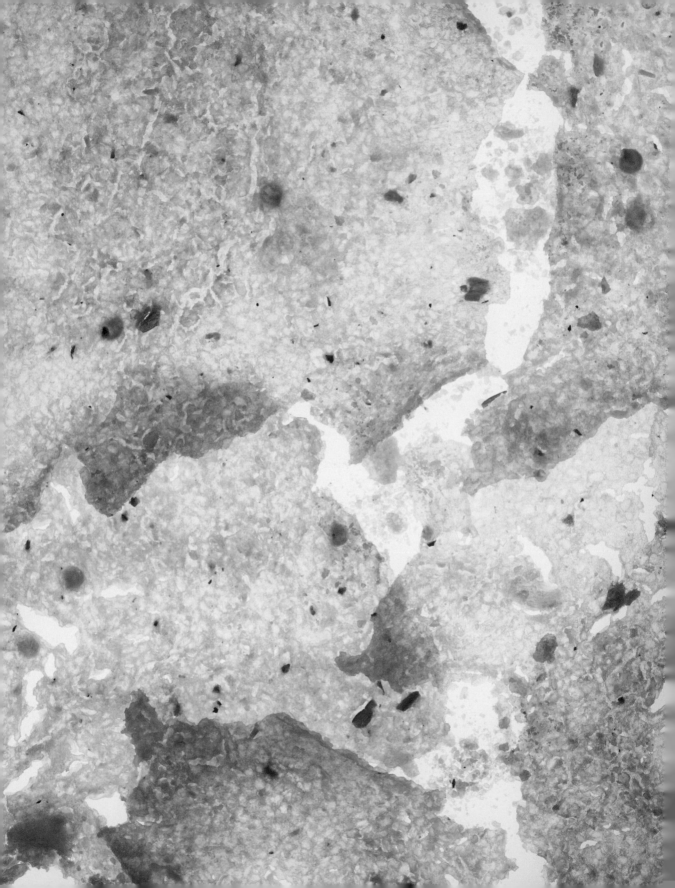

Shrimp and grits is traditionally a stew-y shrimp dish laid atop a soft bed of grits; it's delicious, but hardly an easy dish to take into the woods. After I started experimenting with dried shrimp as a briny, savory, slightly sweet flavor booster, I knew I could make a knockout dish by putting powdered shrimp into a creamy batch of grits. The result takes grits from comforting blandness to thrilling complexity—even better, you can dry the finished dish and reconstitute it easily. It's so good you may want to double the batch and include some in an at-home supper.

ALL-IN-ONE SHRIMP AND GRITS

MAKES 4 SERVINGS

4 cups [960 ml] water

1 cup [190 g] stone-ground corn grits, white or yellow (I like Old School brand)

Fine sea salt

Freshly ground black pepper

½ tsp red pepper flakes, plus more as needed

½ cup [40 g] Dried Shrimp (page 42)

1 Tbsp butter

1. Line dehydrator trays with nonstick fruit-leather sheets.

2. In a large saucepan over medium-high heat, bring the water to a boil. Whisk in the grits and ½ tsp salt and bring back to a boil, whisking constantly. Turn the heat to low and simmer for 20 to 25 minutes, stirring frequently, until the grits are tender. Remove from the heat and stir in ¼ tsp black pepper and the red pepper flakes, dried shrimp, and butter. Taste and adjust the seasoning, if desired. Place a piece of parchment paper on the surface of the grits, and let cool to room temperature.

3. Remove the parchment paper. Spread out the grits mixture very thinly on the prepared trays. **Dry at 135°F [57°C] for 6 to 8 hours,** until completely dry and crackly. Let cool completely. In a spice grinder or a food processor, pulverize to a coarse grind.

4. Store in an airtight container, preferably with a silica gel packet to extend freshness, in a dark place at room temperature for up to 1 month, or in the freezer for up to 6 months.

TO PREPARE 1 SERVING:

In a small pot, stir ⅓ cup [25 g] dried grits into ⅔ cup [160 ml] boiling water. Cover and let sit for about 10 minutes until softened. Uncover and reheat to the desired temperature, stirring often. Add a splash of water and a dash of olive oil, if desired, before serving.

Saffron is just the thing to add a little sunshine into your trail food. It's an expensive spice, to be sure, but just a bit will light up your meals in the wilderness. This delicious rice porridge is a ready-to-pack version of risotto milanese, the traditional accompaniment to osso bucco, or braised veal shanks. It will go well with most stews you might pack in with you. If you like, stir in some green peas (fresh or dried) for color and contrasting flavor.

SAFFRON RISOTTO

MAKES ABOUT 4 SERVINGS

1 tsp saffron threads

Fine sea salt

6 cups [1.4 L] chicken stock

1 Tbsp olive oil

2 Tbsp unsalted butter

1 small onion, finely chopped

2 cups [390 g] short-grained, starchy rice like Arborio or Carnaroli

Pinch of cayenne pepper

½ cup [60 g] freshly grated Parmigiano-Reggiano cheese

1 tsp fresh lemon juice

1. Line dehydrator trays with nonstick fruit-leather sheets.

2. In a dry skillet over medium-low heat, toast the saffron for 1 to 2 minutes, until dry and just a shade darker. Monitor the saffron carefully because it can easily burn. Transfer to a cutting board and let cool. Add a pinch of salt, then press and drag the back of a spoon against the saffron and salt to grind into a fine powder.

3. In a large pot over medium-high heat, bring the chicken stock to a boil, then turn the heat to low and simmer. Add the saffron-salt powder and stir to dissolve.

4. In a wide nonreactive sauce-pan over medium heat, warm the olive oil and 1 Tbsp of the butter. Add the onion and ½ tsp salt, and stir. Cook the onion for 4 to 5 minutes, stirring occasionally, until translucent and fragrant.

5. Add the rice to the pan and stir to coat with the onion mixture. Cook, stirring frequently, for about 2 minutes, until the rice is well coated and a shade more opaque. Add ½ cup [120 ml] of the hot stock and another ½ tsp salt, and stir. When the rice has absorbed the liquid, stir in another ½ cup [120 ml] stock, and stir. Repeat, adding hot stock and stirring whenever the rice has absorbed the preceding addition. Cook for 18 to 20 minutes, stirring often, until the rice is creamy but still retains its form and a little bit of bite. You may not need to add all the stock. Turn off the heat and stir in the cayenne, remaining 1 Tbsp butter, Parmigiano-Reggiano, and lemon juice. Taste and season with salt, if desired. Let cool to room temperature.

6. Spread out the risotto in a thin layer on the prepared trays. (The key for even drying of risotto is to spread not much thicker than a single grain of rice.) **Dry at 145°F [63°C] for 8 to 10 hours,** until crackly dry even on the underside. Let cool completely. Peel the risotto off the sheets, put on a work surface, and crumble.

7. Store in an airtight container, preferably with a silica gel packet to extend freshness, in a dark place at room temperature for up to 1 month, or in the freezer for up to 6 months.

TO PREPARE 1 SERVING:

In a small pot, stir 1 cup [80 g] dried risotto into 1 cup [240 ml] boiling water. Cover and let sit for 15 minutes. Bring to a boil, then turn the heat to low and simmer for 2 to 4 minutes, until the risotto is evenly moist, then let sit for 5 minutes before stirring. Add a bit more hot water for a looser risotto, if desired. You can also brighten up the risotto with additional grated Parmigiano-Reggiano cheese, a pinch of fresh or dried basil, and a bit of lemon juice.

Dried potatoes are very much worth bringing along into the wilderness. And if you work with good potatoes, you'll preserve a lot of delicious flavor that you might not get from packaged mashed potatoes. I kept the reconstitution recipe simple here but, if you want to build on the potatoes, feel free to add some bacon bits, dehydrated sour cream, or sliced onion, which you have dried and brought along (see Dehydration Chart for Common Foods, page 160).

SKILLET POTATOES

MAKES 4 TO 6 SIDE SERVINGS

2 lb [910 g] fingerling potatoes or other small, thin-skinned potatoes

1. Line dehydrator trays with non-stick mesh sheets that have been lightly coated with cooking oil.

2. Slice the potatoes very thinly using a mandoline or a sharp knife. As you work, place the potatoes in a bowl of cool water to prevent discoloring.

3. Bring a large pot of salted water to a boil over medium-high heat. Have ready a bowl of ice water and a spider or slotted spoon. Put about one-third of the potato slices in the pot. Let cook for about 2 minutes, until the potato slices are pliable but still firm. Using the spider, put the blanched potatoes in the ice water. Let the hot water come back to a boil and repeat. Drain the potatoes and spread out on clean kitchen towels to dry.

4. Lay out the potato slices in a single layer on the prepared trays. **Dry at 135°F [57°C] for 7 to 9 hours**, until the potatoes are crackly dry. Let cool completely.

5. Store in airtight containers, preferably with a silica gel packet to extend freshness, in a dark place at room temperature for up to 6 months.

TO PREPARE 1 SERVING:

In a small pot, cover 1 cup [20 g] dried sliced potatoes with boiling water. Cover and let sit for 20 minutes. Drain and blot dry with a clean cloth; the more thoroughly you dry the slices, the better they will brown.

In a frying pan over medium-high heat, warm 1 Tbsp olive oil and sprinkle in fresh or reconstituted dried sliced onions. Cook gently until the onions are soft, but not browned, 4 to 5 minutes. Lay the potatoes in a thin layer across the bottom of the frying pan and season with a pinch of salt and, if desired, some herbes de Provence salt. Cook without stirring for 4 to 5 minutes, until the onions are dark golden brown and the edges of the potato slices are beginning to brown. Flip the potatoes and cook for an additional 4 to 5 minutes, until the edges of many potato slices are crisp and brown. Serve immediately.

Take a stripped-down but delicious hummus recipe, spread it out thin, and then dry it to a rough powder, and you've got a delicious treat for your days in the wilderness. A little lemon zest dried and then tossed into the mix provides a distinct citrus lift. Blended with water, the mix is smooth, creamy, and satisfying as is, but don't be afraid to make it more vivacious with a few treats, if you've packed them in to your campsite, like a squirt of extra-virgin olive oil, a squeeze of fresh lemon, and even a bit of minced fresh garlic. Looking for something to dip in the hummus? Try Za'atar Pita Chips (page 134).

LEMON ZEST HUMMUS FOR THE ROAD

MAKES ABOUT 12 SERVINGS

3 cups [850 g] cooked chickpeas

1 cup [220 g] tahini

3 garlic cloves, peeled and minced

3 Tbsp fresh lemon juice, plus finely grated zest of 1 lemon

1¼ tsp fine sea salt

½ tsp ground cumin

1 cup [240 ml] cold water

1. Line dehydrator trays with nonstick fruit-leather sheets.

2. In a food processor (or blender), pulse the chickpeas a few times, then process steadily to make a chunky paste. Add the tahini, garlic, lemon juice, salt, and cumin and pulse several times to combine. Leaving the motor running, slowly drizzle in the cold water, 2 to 3 Tbsp at a time. Process the hummus until it is very smooth and creamy.

3. Using an offset spatula or the back of a spoon, spread out the hummus as thinly as possible on the prepared trays, then mark an all-over crosshatch pattern in the surface of the hummus to improve surface exposure. Sprinkle the lemon zest on a separate area of one of the prepared trays. **Dry at 125°F [52°C] for 6 to 8 hours**, until the hummus feels dry to the touch and crumbles easily. If you can, you may want to flip the drying hummus

about two-thirds of the way through processing to speed up drying. Let cool completely.

4. Using a food processor (or blender), grind the dried hummus and lemon zest to a fine powder.

5. Store in an airtight container, preferably with a silica gel packet to extend freshness, in a dark place at room temperature for up to 1 month, or in the freezer for up to 6 months.

TO PREPARE 1 SERVING:

In a small bowl, cover ¼ cup [30 g] dried hummus with 3 Tbsp ambient-temperature water. Let sit for about 15 minutes, stirring occasionally. Add more water, 1 tsp at a time, to create your desired consistency.

OTHER USES FOR YOUR DEHYDRATOR

The gentle warmth and circulation of the dehydrator makes it handy for a number of home drying activities that don't quite fit into the preceding chapters. From making yogurt to pet treats to drying craft components, it's usefulness is unlimited!

MAKING YOGURT

Making fresh yogurt gives you wonderful flavor and saves both money and packaging, and a box dehydrator with removable shelves, like the Excalibur models, is a great machine to incubate heat-loving yogurt cultures.

MAKES ABOUT 1 QT [960 ML]

1 qt [960 ml] whole milk

2 Tbsp fresh live-culture plain yogurt, or 1 package freeze-dried yogurt culture

1. Remove the trays from your dehydrator. Warm four 8-oz [240-ml] mason jars in the oven or fill them with hot water for a few minutes.

2. In a heavy-bottomed saucepan over medium-low heat, slowly heat the whole milk. Stir frequently and monitor the temperature. When it reaches 185°F [85°C], remove from the heat and let cool to 115°F [46°C].

3. Whisk in the yogurt; or in a small bowl, whisk a bit of the warm milk with the freeze-dried yogurt culture, and then stir the dissolved culture into the rest of the milk.

4. If you warmed the jars with water, pour out the water and quickly dry with a clean towel. Pour the milk mixture into the warm jars. Place the jars in the dehydrator, uncovered, and run the machine at 100°F [37°C] for 6 to 8 hours, until the yogurt sets. Remove the jars from the dehydrator, cover, and chill for about 2 hours before serving.

CANDYING FLOWERS

Candied flowers are frivolous fun, and perfect ornaments for cupcakes or sugar cookies. They have a delicate flavor (you could add rose water to the egg white wash, if you want to enhance the flavor a little). Use individual petals from roses, or whole pansy or violet blossoms.

MAKES ABOUT 1 CUP [10 G]

1½ Tbsp water

1 tsp rose or orange flower water (optional)

1 egg white

1 cup [200 g] superfine sugar

4 cups [100 g] unsprayed organic, edible flowers or petals, from roses, violets, pansies, borage, pinks (bitter white bits trimmed away), or day lilies

1. Line dehydrator trays with nonstick mesh sheets.

2. In a medium bowl, combine the water and rose water (if using) with the egg white and whisk until frothy. Put the sugar in a shallow bowl. Paint each rose petal front and back with the egg wash and then dip the petals into the sugar, making sure the sugar adheres to the petals on both sides.

3. Place the petals on the prepared trays. Dry at 125°F [52°C] for 12 to 14 hours, until completely dry and crisp. Because the sugar absorbs moisture, these actually dry faster than naked rose petals.

RISING BREAD DOUGH

In the past, I courted disaster by propping rising bread dough on a warm radiator. But with the dehydrator set at 100° to 115°F [37° to 46°C], I can proof bread in a steady, stable place without worry.

Remove all the trays but one from the dehydrator. Place a little dish of water in the bottom of the machine, with the tray above it, and cover your rising dough with a damp towel or oiled plastic wrap. Turn on low (125°F [52°C]) for 60 to 90 minutes.

DRYING PASTA

Next time you make fresh pasta, dry it in single layers on lined dehydrator trays at 135°F [57°C] for 2 to 4 hours, until brittle.

REVIVING STALE CRACKERS

If your crackers could use a little more crispness, you can process them in the dehydrator at around 155°F [68°C] for 30 minutes to 1 hour to restore their crunch.

MAKING DOG TREATS

One of the great beneficiaries of my dehydrator recipe testing was my puppy, who has received many bits of jerky along the way. You don't need to share your jerky, though. Dogs are very happy with simpler bits of dried meats, like liver, lung, or heart. Cut the meat to about double the size you want the finished treat to be and dry at your dehydrator's highest setting.

Follow the basic procedures for drying and storage in the jerky chapter, but skip the marinating step. Keep in mind that lean meats are best for drying. You can also dry vegetables—yams cut into ½-in [12-mm] slices make tasty chewy treats and may be a good choice for dogs with sensitive digestive systems. Dry yam slices at 135°F [57°C] for 6 to 8 hours until leathery.

DRYING BOTANICALS FOR CRAFTS

You can use the food dehydrator to dry leaves, flowers, and stems for craft projects. If you want to keep them flat, try sandwiching what you want to dry between mesh screens. This will also keep petals or other small bits of plant material from whirling around the dehydrator.

DRYING KIDS' ART IN A PINCH

If your kids have been painting and their artworks are still tacky, you can place the artworks on your dehydrator trays and hurry the drying along. Keep the temperature low, around 125°F [52°C].

DEHYDRATION CHART FOR COMMON FOODS

	PREP	DRYING TIME	DEHYDRATOR TEMPERATURE
APPLES	chips: sliced crosswise ⅛ in [3 mm] thick, or thinner	4 to 6 hours	135°F [57°C]
	slices: ⅓-in [6-mm] wedges	6 to 8 hours	135°F [57°C]
APRICOTS	pitted, halved	12 to 24 hours	135°F [57°C]
	whole: slit, pitted	18 to 30 hours	135°F [57°C]
ASPARAGUS	tough ends removed, thinly sliced diagonally	6 to 8 hours	125°F [52°C]
BANANAS	sliced ¼ in [6 mm] thick	14 to 18 hours	135°F [57°C]
BAY SHRIMP	shelled	6 to 10 hours	160° to 165°F [71° to 74°C]
BEETS AND OTHER ROOT VEGETABLES	blanched, peeled, sliced ⅛ in [3 mm] thin	8 to 12 hours	135°F [57°C]
BELL PEPPERS	cored, sliced ¼ in [6 mm] thick or chopped	8 to 10 hours	135°F [57°C]
	roasted: peeled, seeded, quartered	10 to 14 hours	135°F [57°C]
CHERRIES AND SOUR CHERRIES	whole, pitted	24 to 26 hours	135°F [57°C]
CHERRY TOMATOES	blanched till skins crack	18 to 30 hours	135°F [57°C]
CHICKEN	roasted, pulled apart in threads	6 to 10 hours	160° to 165°F [71° to 74°C]
CHICKPEAS	whole	4 to 6 hours	160° to 165°F [71° to 74°C]
CORN	shucked, cut off cob	8 to 12 hours	125°F [52°C]
CROUTONS	1-in [2.5-cm] pieces	3 to 4 hours	160° to 165°F [71° to 74°C]
EGGPLANT	sliced ¼ in [6 mm] thick	4 to 8 hours	125°F [52°C]
FENNEL	sliced ⅛ in [3 mm] thick	12 to 14 hours	135°F [57°C]

DONENESS CUES	OPTIONAL SUGGESTIONS	STORAGE
crisp when cool	dip first to preserve color: 1 tsp citric acid in 4 cups [960 ml] water	keeps for 1 month; but if eaten as a snack, best within 2 to 3 days of drying
dry to touch, springy, still pliable	dip first to preserve color: 1 tsp citric acid in 4 cups [960 ml] water	3 months at room temperature, 1 year in freezer
chewy, leathery, not squishy	dip first to preserve color: 1 tsp citric acid in 4 cups [960 ml] water	3 months at room temperature, 6 months in freezer
leathery, not squishy	dip first to preserve color: 1 tsp citric acid in 4 cups [960 ml] water	3 months at room temperature, 6 months in freezer
brittle		3 months at room temperature, 6 months in freezer
dry to touch, chewy, leathery	dip first to preserve color: 1 tsp citric acid in 4 cups [960 ml] water	3 months at room temperature, 6 months in freezer
crisp, light	grind into powder to add to chili powders and salads, or soak to add to stir fries	1 week at room temperature, 6 months in freezer
leathery	best used for reconstituting in sauces or soups	3 months at room temperature, 6 months in freezer
leathery	best used for reconstituting in sauces or soups	3 months at room temperature, 6 months in freezer
leathery	good for snacking and reconstituting	3 months at room temperature, 6 months in freezer
chewy, not squishy		1 month at room temperature, 1 year in freezer
wrinkled, not squishy		3 months at room temperature, 6 months in freezer
brittle	best used for reconstituting in sauces or soups	1 week in refrigerator, 6 months in freezer
crunchy, darkened		keeps for 1 month; but if eaten as a snack, best within 2 to 3 days of drying
brittle	best used for reconstituting in sauces or soups	3 months at room temperature, 6 months in freezer
crispy, completely dry		1 week at room temperature
leathery	best used for reconstituting in sauces or soups	3 months at room temperature, 6 months in freezer
brittle	dip first to preserve color: 1 tsp citric acid in 4 cups [960 ml] water	3 months at room temperature, 6 months in freezer

	PREP	DRYING TIME	DEHYDRATOR TEMPERATURE
FIGS	halved	12 to 18 hours	135°F [57°C]
	whole: blanched, and/or skin scored	28 to 36 hours	135°F [57°C]
FRUIT LEATHER	puréed fruit, sweetened to taste	4 to 7 hours	135°F [57°C]
GRAPES	blanched till skins crack	16 to 24 hours	135°F [57°C]
HERBS, HEARTY: THYME, OREGANO, ROSEMARY, VERBENA	leave on stem	4 to 8 hours	115° to 125°F [46° to 52°C]
HERBS, TENDER: BASIL, MINT, PARSLEY, TARRAGON	leave on stem, blanch	4 to 6 hours	135°F [57°C]
HUCKLEBERRIES	whole	10 to 12 hours	135°F [57°C]
HUMMUS	spread thin	6 to 8 hours	125°F [52°C]
JALAPEÑO, FRESNO, KOREAN, OR OTHER SMALL HOT CHILES	whole, skin scored	36 to 60 hours	125°F [52°C]
JERKY	thinly sliced (⅛ in [3 mm] thick), salted meat or thinly spread salted ground meat	3 to 5 hours	160° to 165°F [71° to 74°C]
KALE	large stems removed, cut into 2-in [5-cm] slices	5 to 8 hours	135°F [57°C]
KIWI	sliced ¼ in [6 mm] thick	6 to 10 hours	135°F [57°C]
MANGOS	sliced ⅛ in [3 mm] thick	4 to 6 hours	135°F [57°C]
MELON	peeled, seeded, sliced ¼ in [6 mm] thick	8 to 12 hours	135°F [57°C]
MERINGUES	rounded tablespoons	3 to 6 hours	160° to 165°F [71° to 74°C]
MUSHROOMS	stems removed, sliced lengthwise ⅜ in [1 cm] thick	4 to 8 hours	135°F [57°C]
NECTARINES	¼-in [6-mm] wedges	6 to 12 hours	135°F [57°C]
OATMEAL	cooked Irish/Scottish oats	9 to 12 hours	145°F [63°C]
OLIVES	pitted, chopped coarsely	10 to 14 hours	135°F [57°C]

DONENESS CUES	OPTIONAL SUGGESTIONS	STORAGE
leathery, not squishy	if you dry on a nonstick sheet, it takes longer, but cut surface won't get too tough	3 months at room temperature, 6 months in freezer
leathery, not squishy	make sure to work with fruit that is heavy for its size	3 months at room temperature, 6 months in freezer
leathery, dry on top and bottom	spread thin on nonstick sheets, thicker at edges	2 weeks at room temperature, 1 month in the refrigerator.
wrinkled, leathery, not squishy	there will often be a handful of grapes that don't feel leathery; eat them soon, rather than storing	3 months at room temperature, 6 months in freezer
crumbly leaves	remove from stem when dry	3 months at room temperature
crumbly leaves	remove from stem when dry	3 months at room temperature
chewy	4 oz [115 g] huckleberries yields ½ oz [15 g]	3 months at room temperature, 6 months in freezer
cracked, dry throughout	turn over and crumble during drying to ensure complete dryness	1 month at room temperature, 6 months in freezer
leathery and hollow sounding		6 months at room temperature
dry, leathery, but still pliable	blot with paper towels while cooling	1 week at room temperature, 2 weeks in refrigerator, 6 months in freezer
crackly dry		keeps for 1 month; but if eaten as a snack, best within 2 to 3 days of drying
leathery		3 months at room temperature, 6 months in freezer
leathery		3 months at room temperature, 6 months in freezer
dense, springy, chewy		3 months at room temperature, 6 months in freezer
airy, crisp		1 month at room temperature
airy, brittle		6 months at room temperature
leathery	dip first to preserve color: 1 tsp citric acid in 4 cups [960 ml] water	3 months at room temperature, 6 months in freezer
crackly dry	turn over toward end of drying to ensure complete dryness	1 month at room temperature, 6 months in freezer
crisp-edged	delicious as seasoning on top of soups, salads, pastas	3 months at room temperature

	PREP	DRYING TIME	DEHYDRATOR TEMPERATURE
ONIONS	peeled, sliced thinly	8 to 12 hours	125°F [52°C]
PEACHES	pitted, quartered or halved	20 to 36 hours	135°F [57°C]
PEAS	shucked, blanched, or from frozen	6 to 10 hours	125°F [52°C]
PEARS	cored, quartered	8 to 16 hours	135°F [57°C]
PINEAPPLE	peeled, quartered, cored, cut into ½-in [12-mm] pieces	16 to 24 hours	135°F [57°C]
PITA CHIPS	tossed with olive oil	3 to 4 hours	160° to 165°F [71° to 74°C]
PLUMS	halved, pitted	18 to 36 hours	135°F [57°C]
POTATOES	sliced ⅛ in [3 mm] thick on mandoline, blanched	6 to 8 hours	135°F [57°C]
QUINOA	cooked, spread thin on nonstick sheet	6 to 8 hours	135°F [57°C]
RASPBERRIES	whole	18 to 24 hours	135°F [57°C]
ROSE PETALS	separated, picked over for dirt and bugs	36 to 48 hours	125°F [52°C]
SALMON JERKY	sliced ¼ in [6 mm] thick on bias	5 to 8 hours	160° to 165°F [71° to 74°C]
SPINACH	blanched	4 to 6 hours	135°F [57°C]
STRAWBERRIES	sliced ⅛ in [3 mm] thick	8 to 12 hours	135°F [57°C]
	quartered	14 to 16 hours	135°F [57°C]
TOMATOES	petals: peeled, quartered, seeded, cored	2 to 4 hours	135°F [57°C]
	slices: ⅛ in [3 mm] thick	14 to 18 hours	135°F [57°C]
WINTER SQUASH	roasted, puréed, spread on nonstick sheets	7 to 11 hours	135°F [57°C]
ZUCCHINI	thinly sliced	3 to 5 hours	135°F [57°C]

DONENESS CUES	OPTIONAL SUGGESTIONS	STORAGE
crisp but a bit chewy	smelly; work in well-ventilated space	1 month at room temperature, 6 months in freezer
leathery, not squishy		3 months at room temperature, 6 months in freezer
brittle	best used for reconstituting in sauces or soups	6 months at room temperature
chewy	dip first to preserve color: 1 tsp citric acid in 4 cups [960 ml] water	3 months at room temperature, 6 months in freezer
chewy, not squishy		3 months at room temperature, 1 year in freezer
completely crisp		2 weeks at room temperature
leathery, not squishy	check plum on skin side; when fully dried, it will not wiggle when poked	3 months at room temperature, 6 months in freezer
dry, brittle		6 months at room temperature
crumbly		1 month at room temperature, 6 months in freezer
dry to touch, chewy	best used for infusions or reconstituting in sauces	3 months at room temperature, 6 months in freezer
dry, brittle	let sit before removing from dryer; they often need more time than you think	6 months at room temperature
dry to touch, still pliable	blot with paper towels while cooling	2 weeks in refrigerator, 6 months in freezer
brittle	best used for reconstituting in sauces or soups; can be ground into powder to use as coloring	3 months at room temperature, 6 months in freezer
leathery-crisp		3 months at room temperature, 6 months in freezer
chewy		3 months at room temperature, 6 months in freezer
soft, dense, chewy		2 to 3 days, or up to 1 week covered with oil, in refrigerator
leathery-crisp		3 months at room temperature, 6 months in freezer
leathery	best dissolved in soups and stews	3 months at room temperature, 6 months in freezer
crisp, a bit chewy	larger zucchini, which tend to be dry, work best	keeps for 1 month; but if eaten as a snack, best within 2 to 3 days of drying

INDEX